HISTORIC SPORTING CAMPS OF MOOSEHEAD LAKE, MAINE

Copyright © 2023

Roger Allen Moody

ISBN: 978-1-943424-80-1

LCCN: 2023938947

All rights reserved. No part of this book may be reproduced in any form or by any electronic or mechanical means, including information storage and retrieval systems, without permission in writing from the author, except by a reviewer, who may quote brief passages in review.

Photo credits: Shown by each image.

Printed in the United States of America

North Country Press
Unity, Maine

Cover: Camp Greenleaf main lodge on Sugar Island ca 1906. Image courtesy of the Moosehead Historical Society 2001.23.0

i

Contents

Contents ii

Acknowledgements iv

Preface v

Rise of Sporting Camps in the Post-Civil War Era 1

Women at Sporting Camps 5

Steamboats and Communications 10

Railroads and Automobiles 17

Fishing and Hunting Resources 20

Guides 29

Leased Land 38

Forestland Conservation 39

Watercraft, Snowmobiles, ATVs, and Mountain Bikes 42

Sporting Camps Today and Tomorrow 44

Index to Camp Locations 48

Camp Allagash -The Crow's Nest 50

Beaver Cove Camps 54

The Birches 58

The Capen's 63

Camps Caribou - Whileaway - Ogontz 69

Folsom Farm 98

Gilbert & Coombs - West Outlet Camps - Old Mill Campground
.... 102

Gray Ghost Camps 106

Camps Greenleaf - Sugar Island -Thorofare - Moosehead - Porcupine - Wilderness Lodge - Eagle Haven 110

Kokad-Jo Inn - Roach River House - Kokadjo Cabins & Trading Post 125

Lily Bay House 134

Marr's Indian Pond Camps 140

Maynard's in Maine 144

Miller's Training Camp 150

Mt. Kineo Hotel and Resort 157

Northern Pride Lodge 169

Northeast Carry - The Penobscot Hotel 173

Northeast Carry - Winnegarnock House & Supply Store - Raymond's Country Store 176

Northwest Carry - Seboomook House - Seboomook Campground 187

Randall's Camps - Chadwick's Camps - West Branch Pond Camps 196

Second Roach Pond Camps – Medawisla 201

Spencer Bay Camps - Casey's Campground 205

Spencer Pond Camps 209

Squaw Mountain Inn - Moose Mountain Inn 214

Tomhegan Camps 218

Wheat's Island Camps 225

Whitten's Store - Moosehead Inn and Cabins - Whitten's Cottages - Whitten's Lodge & Cabins 227

Wilson's East Outlet Camps 235

Private Sporting Clubs 242

Lakeside Housekeeping Cabins & Campgrounds 261

Reference Resources and Index 270

Acknowledgements

The process of writing this book was inspired and supported by those individuals who appreciate Maine history and love to learn more about it. Their contributions are acknowledged with deep gratitude.

The Moosehead Historical Society and Museum's Executive Director Suzanne AuClair, staff members Mary Stefanik and Andrea Johns, and volunteer Barbara Crossman.

William Geller, historian, researcher, and author, whose most recent works are W*ithin Katahdin's Realm: Log Drives and Sporting Camps* and *West of Chesuncook & North of Moosehead: Maine Log Drives & Sporting Camps, 1830-1971.* Bill's support for the concept of this book and suggestions for resource documents provided the foundation for much of the research contained herein. His review of a near-final draft provided invaluable assistance in making needed corrections.

Those who read individual chapters, and provided additional information and corrections: Craig Hadley, Kokadjo, Annie Finch, Richard Brautigam, Tom and Dianne Folsom, Gail Maynard, Virginia McCabe-Crumb, Steve and Amy Lane, Donald A. Wilson, Nat Fleck, Roy and Susie Landau Finch, and Marta and Charles Kozlosky.

Desiree Butterfield-Nagy, M.L.I.S., Special Collections Department, Raymond H. Fogler Library, University of Maine, Orono, for research assistance.

My spouse Audrey Simpson Moody for her research assistance and proofreading skills that significantly improved the quality of this book.

Preface

As a long-term Moosehead Lake camp owner, I've often wondered about the histories of the sporting camps on the lake. How have these camps responded to the economic, technological, and cultural changes brought by the passage of time from the post-Civil War era to that of the present day; to the changes from transportation by stage, railroads, and steamers to road networks and automobiles; to the 40-hour work week and increases in leisure time; to the impact of "back to nature" movements; and to the cultural favor or disfavor of hunting and fishing? These questions begged for exploration.

Through the decades, Moosehead Lake has remained an attraction for individuals and families who seek hunting, fishing, outdoor sports, hiking, recreation, and renewal in an environment of clean waters, spectacular mountains, and the challenges of experiences in the great north woods.

The intended geographic scope of this book is to trace those sporting camps located on Moosehead Lake itself, on the Moose River to the Brassua Lake Dam, the Roach River, Spencer Stream tributaries, and the tip of Indian Pond at the confluence of Moosehead Lake's east and west outlets.

Some of the former camps no longer exist, of course, their sites having been sold and converted into private family property or residential subdivisions. Others are for sale with their futures undetermined at this point.

The earliest stories of the various camps are told partly through copies of their advertisements from publications which focused on Maine woods and waters, because they typically featured the services and experiences available to "sports" and guests.

Fortunately, some historic sporting camps have evolved from the mid-1880s and continue to exist today, and newer ones have been developed over the decades. From economic necessity, all current camps, even those that have existed for 100 years or more, place increased emphasis on recreational and outdoor experiences aside from hunting and fishing. They have thrived by adjusting and evolving over the years to offer customer services and experiences which reflect social and cultural trends, and the ongoing development of new technologies.

For many contemporary visitors to camps, their experiences with "sporting" camps relate to annual vacations, renewed friendships, and enhanced appreciation for nature and the outdoors. Opportunities to shun electronic media creates times for conversation, storytelling, reading, and board games, especially during evenings in lodges or around campfires.

Roger Allen Moody

Rise of Sporting Camps in the Post-Civil War Era

Buoyed by his travel experiences in Maine's North Woods in the mid-1800s, Henry David Thoreau wrote widely about the values of nature appreciation, and the physical and psychological renewal brought by life in the outdoors. That philosophy helped draw "rusticators" and "sports" to Maine's lakes, streams, mountains, and the vast north woods from throughout the eastern United States during the post-Civil War era and extending to the 1930s.

The Civil War, although filled with stresses and perils, led to the development of new sources of wealth which led the nation into an era of material prosperity. It generated a new appreciation for the outdoors as evidenced by W.H.H. Murray and crusades for the "gospel of rest." (William Henry Harrison Murray (1840–1904), also known as "Adirondack Murray," was an American clergyman and author of an influential series of articles and books which popularized the Adirondack Mountains in upstate New York. He became known as the father of the Outdoor Movement. In 1869, his lectures about the Adirondacks were published as a book, *Adventures in the Wilderness; or Camp-Life in the Adirondacks*.)

Lucius Hubbard's introductory comments, in his 1893 *Hubbard's Guide to Moosehead Lake and Northern Maine*, reflected these themes. "To the care-worn businessman and overworked student, no relaxation from the constant wear of their respective callings is so grateful as that which comes while camping in the woods. ... In the wild woods life is regenerated, and even after two weeks of camping out and canoeing one issues forth with renewed strength for the work of the coming year. Rest and relaxation are an absolute necessity."

Rise of Sporting Camps in the Post-Civil War Era

In the late nineteenth century, a new, increasingly urban, middle class emerged that had more leisure time and disposable income than common people had ever enjoyed before. Eager to spend their income and newfound time outside the workplace, the middle class turned to the outdoors and sports, either as participants or spectators.

The sporting camps responded to the evolution in upper-class and middle-class attitudes toward nature, the perceptions of the value of leisure time, and the positive impact of outdoor activities on health. Men, women, and children, primarily from urban centers on the east coast, looked to Maine, among other places, for vacations. Maine sporting camps provided the services and skills necessary to experience nature at a primeval level, but at the same time offered a degree of the comforts clients customarily enjoyed in their urban settings.

There were four identifiable categories of sporting camps. First, classic sporting camps were defined by their remote locations, distinctive log-built architecture, and lack of electricity. The more remote and spartan accommodations often offered greater game and fish resources, and guests could pursue outdoor oriented sports like hiking, canoeing, and wildlife observation. Secondly, the luxurious sporting camps that were actually resorts, such as the Mt. Kineo Hotel, offered sporting vacations of complete comfort with many social events. A third, small, category of sporting camps consisted of operations run out of remote houses and farms. The fourth category was composed of private hunting and fishing "clubs" whose membership and facilities were primarily for businessmen.

As conceptualized in popular travel literature, classic camps included a central dining lodge with surrounding cabins for the guests, owners, and guides. The cabins were spaced apart to afford some privacy for the guests, but they were close enough to create a small, self-contained community in the wilderness. Camps had to be located near areas with wildlife and lake access, as many daily activities revolved around hunting and fishing. Prices for sporting

Rise of Sporting Camps in the Post-Civil War Era

camp vacations started at several dollars per day and increased with the amount of luxury. Sports hired knowledgeable guides to escort them into the wilderness and to ensure their safety and success in these pursuits.

Classic sporting camp operations often included a whole family with proprietor's wives cooking the meals. The camps were generally too remote to regularly serve food items that the clients expected, and families worked their nearby farms to supply fresh vegetables and fruit, and tended chickens and domestic animals.

Camp proprietors and guides often built branch camps, too; small cabin a day away from the main camps, to enable sports to get to the best fishing and hunting locations.

"Sports" and guides at Maynard's in Maine. maynardsinmaine.com.

The trains, steamboats, and stagecoaches of the Victorian era formed the transportation infrastructure that made travel to the Maine wilderness possible. During the summer of 1873, for example, Teddy Roosevelt, then a young teenager, made his first trip to Moosehead Lake from New York with his family. They traveled overnight by train to Dexter, Maine, and then boarded a stagecoach for Greenville, from which steamboats took them to their sporting camp destinations.

Rise of Sporting Camps in the Post-Civil War Era

During 1880s and 1890s, the national rail and lake steamer transportation improvements extended into the rural and forested areas of Maine and led to the multiplication of sporting camps. The Bangor and Aroostook Railroad (B&A) extended a rail line to Greenville in 1884 and the Canadian Pacific (CP) from Montreal reached Greenville in 1888. Work began on the Somerset Railroad in 1877 to extend it from Waterville/Oakland, Maine, to Rockwood on Moosehead Lake, a project which was completed in 1906. Guests arriving from urban areas by railroad in either Greenville or Rockwood then traveled via buckboard, stagecoach, lake steamer, or even canoe, to the sporting camp itself.

The Progressive Era (1896–1916) was a period of widespread social activism and political reform across the United States that spanned the 1890s to World War I. The main objectives of the Progressive movement were to address problems caused by industrialization: the pressures of urban growth, immigration, and political corruption. Industrial employers also began to decrease working hours and institute a Saturday half-day schedule, which gave workers more free time for leisure activities. The monotony of specialized industrial work and the crowding of urban expansion created a desire in workers to have leisure time away from their jobs and the intensity of city living. Vacations began to be consistently offered to workers, although they were initially unpaid.

The guests at sporting camps varied according to the time of year. The early spring and late fall months attracted a predominantly male clientele who devoted all their time to fishing (early spring) or to hunting (late fall). During the summer months, when the weather and travel were more agreeable, entire families patronized the camps. With improvements in rail transportation, especially, the number of women increased during all seasons. Indeed, women were actively involved with hunting and fishing by the 1890s.[1]

Women at Sporting Camps

Maine native Cornelia T. Crosby (1854-1946), or "Fly Rod" as she was popularly known, once caught 200 trout by fly rod in a single day; she was also an early advocate of catch-and-release. She was the first woman to legally shoot a caribou in Maine. The love and focus of her writings were hunting and fishing in Maine's north woods, and she worked tirelessly to promote outdoor recreation in Maine to sportsmen and their families.

The local newspaper in Fly Rod's hometown of Phillips, Maine, was the *Phillips Phonograph,* for which Crosby served as a part-time correspondent. By 1893, she was also writing for the national weekly *Shooting and Fishing* and was the subject of a glowing article in the *Chicago Evening Post.* As a travel writer for the Maine Central Railroad Company, Crosby contributed importantly to recreation, sport, and tourism in Maine's wilderness through her popular outdoor column "Fly Rod's Notebook" that was published in the *Maine Woods* magazine and appeared in many newspapers across the United States. The "Fly Rod's Notebook" column typically contained commentary about the guides, camp owners,

Cornelia "Fly Rod" Crosby, 1894. Collections of the Maine State Museum (69.23.1).

camp visitors, and fishing and hunting activity observed as she circulated among many sporting camps. Crosby primarily focused on the Rangeley lakes area of western Maine, but also wrote of Moosehead Lake.

The publicity she generated in her position as a prominent female figure in turn-of-the-century New England, helped to attract thousands of would-be outdoorsmen - and women - to the woods, lakes, and streams of Maine. Her readers were typically wealthy sportsmen and their families who came to Maine for pleasure and relaxation.

In March 1897, the Maine legislature passed a bill requiring hunting guides to register with the state. Fly Rod was the first licensed guide of the 1,316 guides who registered during that year. Crosby once wrote, "I am a plain woman of uncertain age, standing six feet in my stockings. I scribble a bit for various sporting journals, and I would rather fish any day than go to heaven."[2]

Women were actively involved with hunting and fishing by the 1890s. The wives of sportsmen who fished, hunted, and vacationed at Maine sporting camps were encouraged by Crosby to come with their husbands. In 1915, she wrote in "Fly Rod's Notebook," "The wonderful skill which many women show with little practice with rod and rifle; the keen enjoyment they have in coming into our wilderness, where they always find good health awaits them; where they soon forget the gay society life for the real happiness, prove they make good companions. It used to be thought out of place for a woman to join a party going off with guides for a few days, or weeks, but now more parties have women than go without them."[3]

Fly Rod excelled at outdoors sports and was a role model to young women around the nation, bolstering a personal philosophy of athleticism and independence not often found in other women of her time.

Women at Sporting Camps

Aside from her columns and work as a guide, Crosby gained a significant level of fame for her Maine sporting camp exhibit at the New York Sportsman's Exposition in 1895 at Madison Square Garden, in which she displayed an authentic hunting camp including a small log cabin. That exposition was followed in future years with similar events in Boston and Philadelphia.

In the Pine-Tree Jungles. A handbook for sportsmen and campers in the Great North Woods published in 1902, Mary Alden Hopkins wrote an article titled "Women in the Woods," which was a publicity piece to attract women to the outdoors. In it she said,

> "In many a camp one will find a party of women, or group of schoolgirls with their teacher, who tramp and climb and fish under the guardianship of trustworthy Indian guides. A woman who has once experienced the freedom of such a vacation never willingly returns to a seaside hotel veranda. The number who distribute venison of their own shooting among friends at home is increasing each year, and not a few have a lordly moose to their credit. But if a woman does not care for hunting, she explores the wonderful lakes and streams in a canoe, or takes long tramps, from which she returns with an appetite which would appall any but an experienced camp cook. There are fish for the fisherwoman to catch, ferns and orchids for the botanist to classify, and invigorating air and glorious scenery for all to enjoy. ... The Maine forest is a place where sick women grow well, and well women accumulate muscle and happiness; it is a sanitorium, playground, hunting and fishing ground all in one. The good effects of an outing here inevitably prove to be long and lasting, while the joys of the vacation are retained in sweetest memory for the rest of one's life."

Outdoorswoman Fannie Hardy Eckstorm (1865–1946) was an American writer, historian, and folklorist whose extensive personal knowledge of her native state of Maine secured her place as one of the foremost authorities on the history, wildlife, cultures, and lore of the region.

Women at Sporting Camps

Eckstorm authored an article directed to husbands in the 1906 edition of *In the Maine Woods* titled "Take 'Her' with You." (p 81):

"… And yet there is little need today in camping in the Maine woods to overtax even a delicate woman. As for illnesses, unless one brings them with her, they do not come. She won't get ill, not even by sleeping on boughs under a tent in hard fall rains, not even from wind and snow. Don't fret about her health. You think she doesn't care for this sort of life. It is an acquired taste, remember, even with yourself. She hesitates because she is not sure whether she will like it, and her not liking might spoil your whole outing. She fears she would be a burden; she thinks she might prevent your taking the long hard trip which you have been planning; she pre-supposes that if you are after large game you could not be bothered with a woman in the camp; in short, sir, she consults your imagined pleasure rather than her own.

Picnic party at dinner, first falls, Socatean Stream, Sept. 7.1885. Moosehead Lake. Library of Congress, lccn.loc.gov/2002711547.

Women at Sporting Camps

First Socatean Falls and Pool. Hubbard, Lucius L., *Hubbard's Guide to Moosehead Lake and Northern Maine*, Fifth Edition, revised and enlarged edition of "Summer vacations at Moosehead Lake and Vicinity," published by the author, Cambridge, Massachusetts 1893. p 62.

Another aspect of women's roles at sporting camps was that of management, notes Maine historian William Geller. Between 1890 and 1910, as the number of "sports" increased, individual guides opened camps where they could stay. "By 1910, their camps could not survive on just men. The owners turned to their wives for their cooking, ingenuity, and organizational skills. Their love of the wilderness and their work matched that of their husbands. ... This was a notable contrast to the rugged-male omnipresence at the birth of the sporting camp era." [4]

Steamboats and Communications

As the nineteenth century got underway, an exciting advance was the steamboat. What was needed on Moosehead Lake were boats that could both tow large rafts or "booms" of logs to the lake's east outlet

In the Maine Woods ad, 1901.

despite rough weather. In 1836, a logger, dam builder, and river driver by the name of Hogan built the first steamboat on the lake. Early records aren't clear, but she appears to have been named *Moosehead* (thus making her the *Moosehead I*) and to have been 96' long with a 40 hp, low-pressure, steam engine.[5]

In the early 1840s, Major Benjamin Bigney arrived in Greenville from Pugwash, Nova Scotia. He married Lydia Scammon, daughter of an early settler, and settled down to build steamboats. In 1846, he built the side-wheeler *Amphitrite*; in 1858 the *Fairy of the Lake*; and in 1860 *Moosehead II*.[6]

The lake was a natural avenue into the north woods, and those forests were, in turn, a principle economic resource of the state of Maine. Each fall an army of loggers, along with all the supplies and horses needed to support their work during the upcoming winter, was ferried up the lake from Greenville to busy disembarkation wharves at Lily Bay, Seboomook, and Northeast Carry. Come spring, steamers towed harvested logs to the lake's east outlet to be sluiced down the Kennebec. The growing sporting camp business provided an added source of revenue, and during the spring trout-fishing season, steamers catered to sports by day and, with a second crew, towed logs at night.[7]

The quantity and weight of what the steamboats could transport was augmented by using barges towed alongside the boats, or behind when the weather was rough. Scows varied from 60' to 80' in length and 18' to 20' in width, and carried loads of grain, hay, cattle, automobiles, and tons of cement for the Great Northern Paper Company dams.

During the last half of the 19th century, as many as 55 steamboats plied the waters of Moosehead Lake, ferrying supplies to lumber camps, towing log booms, and transporting passengers to sporting camp accommodations and outdoor pursuits.

Passenger steamboats. In the first decades of the 20th Century, the regular routes of the Coburn Steamship Co. were from either the Bangor & Aroostook Railroad terminus in Greenville or the Maine

Steamboats and Communications

Central Railroad's Kineo Station in Rockwood to Deer and Sugar Islands, Lily Bay, Seboomook (Northwest Carry), and Northeast Carry.

> *Milton G. Shaw (1820-1903) was a prominent entrepreneur in Greenville's history. Although he was a significant timberlands owner in the forestlands east of Moosehead Lake, he also owned several steamers, was an investor in the Mt. Kineo resort, and owned the Lily Bay House. He owned the D.T. Sanders Store in Greenville, as well, which in the mid-1800s was the largest general store in Maine.*

Other steamers, such as the *Priscilla* and *Henry M.*, had regular routes (wind and weather permitting), as detailed in this ad.

In the Maine Woods ad, 1901.

The *Henry M.*'s route frequently ran between Greenville Junction and Lily Bay for passengers who then travelled by buckboard to and from other camps near Kokadjo, along the Roach River and the chain of Roach Ponds. Charles Capen of The Capen's captained the Shaw steamboat *Henry M.* during the late 1890s.[8]

Stops were made at the Greenleaf Camps and the Nighthawk Club on Sugar Island, and the Allagash Camps/Crow's Nest Camps at Burnt Jacket on Moosehead's eastern shore.

Steamers were also available for fishing charters.

Steamers *Louisa* and *Cora Lee*

These fast and commodious steamers, entirely overhauled and rebuilt, will be ready for the spring fishing as soon as the ice leaves Moosehead Lake. . . . .
No better boats on the Lake for the comfort of fishing parties. Can be hired by the day or week. Address . . . .

Capt. HENRY P. SAWYER,

GREENVILLE, - - - **MAINE.**

In the Maine Woods ad, 1901.

Fairy of the Lake was typical of the large side-wheelers that were to ply the lake for years. Although she towed log booms and hauled freight for the Coburn Steamboat Co., she had special amenities for passengers and the summer trade.

THE FINE STEAMER

"FAIRY OF THE LAKE,"

Capt. LEWIS GILL,

Will make Regular Daily Trips during the Summer season between Greenville, Mt. Kineo, and Head of Lake, connecting at Greenville with stages each way, to and from Blanchard.

The "FAIRY" has been rebuilt and thoroughly overhauled, and is one of the most popular boats on the Lake. Reasonable terms to Excursion Parties. Address,

J. H. EVELETH,
Greenville, Maine.

Farrar's Illustrated Guidebook to Moosehead Lake and Vicinity ad, 1893.

Steamboats and Communications

The *Fairy of the Lake* was a side-paddle steamboat built in 1853 for John Eveleth and was 140' in length and with a 25' beam amidships

> *John Henry Eveleth was born in 1826 in Monson, Maine, and died in Greenville in 1899, and was a man of unbounded energy throughout his entire lifetime. He found mostly successes in many businesses, with the key to his success to be found in his diversified entrepreneurial spirit. He was a grocery and hardware store owner, owner and investor in timberlands, a lumber mill owner in a family-run operation, and owner of three steamboats and stockholder in others. He was the Greenville postmaster for 21 years, and served the town as selectman, town clerk, and town treasurer.*

where the paddle wheel shaft was located. She had gangways fore and aft, two decks, and could carry 300 people. With her 200 hp engine, she could make eight to ten miles an hour. For 23 years she had a busy life on the lake.[9]

"Line boats" were built to carry passengers, small freight, and the United States mail. These boats ran the lake from Greenville to Seboomook, stopping at a number of resorts, camps, and logging depots. They carried everything from tons upon tons of hay to a spool of thread, and from ice out until the lake froze these boats were the connection to the outside world.

GNP Co.'s monthly magazine *The Northern*, July 1926, reported the names of the steamboats that were frequently transporting sportsmen and timber harvesting machinery to Lily Bay: *Louisa, Ripple, Tethys, Henry M., Comet, Priscilla, Fairy of the Lake, Solano, Julia, Twilight, Rebecca,* and the yacht *Idler*.

Smaller steamboats, often launched as private craft, were more closely involved in the daily lives of residents around the lake. Some sporting camps owned steamboats and launches as transport to bring clients to and from railroad connections in Greenville or Rockwood, for providing excursions on the lake, and for taking the canoes and guides to sites for fishing. For example, the Mt. Kineo Resort had the steam yachts *Day Dream, Kineo, The Patsy*, and the *George A.*; The Capen's had *Tethys I and II*; Tomhegan's was *Rosemary Girl*; the West Outlet Camps owned the launch *West Outlet,* and Wilson's the *East Outlet.*

Camp Caribou pier.
Richard Kessler collection.

Crib pier construction detail.
Burgess Construction, Rangeley, Maine.

The 110' wharf at Camp Caribou (at left) is typical of those at which steamers stopped with passengers and freight. The angled sides allowed the expanding winter ice to ride-up the wharf's sides rather than push the structure pieces, and also dissipated some wave energy from summer storms. They were built as log cribs and filled with stone. A few still exist in exposed locations where floating dock systems wouldn't survive the impact of waves and ice.

Post Offices. Early mail deliveries were made in the summer by steamboats, and across the ice by horse and ice sleds during the winter. During late fall before the lake ice was solidly frozen, or when mud season arrived, loggers or anyone traveling overland north from Greenville would be asked to carry mail. Having a Post Office at a sporting camp was an important amenity which allowed sports and guests to maintain communications with their homes, offices, and businesses, and figured prominently in their advertisements.

Post Offices were located at Mt. Kineo Hotel 1884-1938; Lily Bay 1890-1921, Roach River/Kokadjo 1895-1966; Seboomook 1895-1923; Northeast Carry, beginning in 1889; The Capen's (Deer Island) year-round 1889-1938 and summers only from 1938-1943; Tarratine, serving Marr's Indian Pond Camps 1902-1950; Sugar Island (summer only) 1905-1942; the Kineo & Oakland and Rockwood & Oakland Railway Post Office (RPO) 1906-1933; West Outlet Camps' service began 1914; Ogontz (summer/fall only) 1928-1956.[10]

The Birches' service appears to have started in 1937.

Telegraph. Hubbard's 1893 *Guide to Moosehead Lake and Northern* Maine reported that year-round telegraph services were then available in Greenville, at the Mt. Kineo House, and at Wilson's east outlet camps. Telegraph was available at the Penobscot House at Northeast Carry in 1901.

Telephone. Telephone service was available at the Mt. Kineo Hotel in 1884, and a line was run from Kineo along the eastern shore of the lake to the Winnegarnock House at Northeast Carry in 1897-98, and to Northwest Carry about 1899. Maynard's in Maine advertised both daily mail service and telephone service by 1919. Telephone and telegraph reached Sugar Island about 1925.

Railroads and Automobiles

The arrival of railroad service to Moosehead Lake made comfortable and predictable travel to sporting camps a reality and spurred their growth. In July 1884, the Bangor and Piscataquis Railroad line reached Greenville's West Cove at the southern end of Moosehead Lake. It soon became part of the Bangor and Aroostook Railroad (B&A) system, whose tracks went to the West Cove wharf where tourists climbed aboard Coburn Company or sporting camp steamboats to go up the lake to their vacation destinations.

In 1888, the Canadian Pacific Railroad (CP) came near the western shore of Moosehead Lake at Greenville from Montreal, Quebec, on its way to St. John, New Brunswick. The proximity of the two tracks in Greenville led to the designation of the name Greenville Junction for the West Cove location at the southern end of the lake. B&A and CP passengers could leave either train at the Greenville Junction wharf to take steamboats to their sporting camp or resort.

The Somerset Railroad was chartered in 1860 to build a line north along the Kennebec River from the Maine Central Railroad center at Oakland, Maine, to Rockwood (also known as Birch Point) on Moosehead Lake. Construction reached from Norridgewock to North Anson in 1877, but the company defaulted in 1879. It was then reorganized as the standard gauge Somerset Railway in 1884, and construction continued to Solon in 1889 and Bingham in 1890.

The reorganized Somerset Railroad company extended the rail line to Rockwood in 1906 to serve the expanding 200-room Mt. Kineo Hotel and Resort and the other resorts or sporting camps on the lake. The train had fifteen plush, upholstered coaches, nine baggage cars, and twelve combination smoking-baggage cars with leather seats in the smoking sections.[11]

Railroads and Automobiles

Coburn Wharf, Greenville Junction. Facebook.com/MooseheadMemories/photos

Hotel patrons arrived on overnight Pullman sleeper cars from large eastern cities and reached the Mt. Kineo Hotel by steamboat from the railroad terminal at "Kineo Station" in Rockwood.

The Maine Central Railroad purchased the Mt. Kineo House and Resort along with the Somerset Railway in 1911, and the railway became the Kineo branch of the Maine Central Railroad.[12]

The ownership of motor vehicles grew rapidly in the 1920s, however, and the State Route 15 roadway from Bangor to Rockwood was completed in 1927. Travel soon shifted away from railroads and steamers to the more flexible and personal automobile which enabled families to travel further in less time. As fewer people wanted to escape to the north woods for summerlong vacations, the shorter one-week or two-week vacation became the new norm.

Railroads and Automobiles

E.E. Clement photo contributed by David Larrabee.
Facebook.com/MooseheadMemories/photos

The left side of the image above shows Maine Central's Somerset Railway tracks and wharf at Kineo Station about 1910, with the steamship wharf and railroad station at right; the Kineo House is visible in the distance across Moosehead Lake. Regularly scheduled passenger train service over the Somerset rail line ended on September 6, 1960.

The station buildings and rails were cleared from site, and it became an automobile parking lot for the Mt. Kineo House in the 1940s and 50s. Today it serves as parking lot for the adjacent public boat launch ramps and the Kineo Shuttle which transport hikers and golfers to the Kineo peninsula.

Fishing and Hunting Resources

Fish. In the days before conservation and fish and game limits, it was common for two fishermen to catch four or five hundred pounds of trout and togue during their stay.

In 1894, the legal weight limit was set at 50 lbs. of trout per person per day. Increasing fishing pressure caused this limit to be reduced several times during the coming years, and the limit was 15 lbs. per person in 1908 and remained there until around 1940. Fishing was good on Moosehead Lake throughout this period, and many guides verified that there were few days when the 15 lb. limit was not reached. Many good-sized fish (particularly salmon and togue) were released by their sports.

Almost all the fishing in the early days was done from canoes that were towed in the morning from a sporting camp by the camp's launch. At the fishing grounds, sports clambered into the canoes and fished while their guides slowly paddled them back. Sports typically held rods baited with minnows or streamer flies.

Collection of The Moosehead Historical Society #1995.4.293.

Fishing and Hunting Resources

Given the number of guests that could be accommodated by the area's hotels and sporting camps, steamboats or the camp launches were often used to shuttle excursion trips to various bays and islands around the lake.

As improved roads and more widespread use of automobiles made traveling to Greenville easier in the 1930s, more fishermen came to the lake and the number of fish in the lake began to decline. The daily weight limit was reduced to 7½ pounds in 1942. The post-World War II years provided Moosehead with a brief reprieve from angling pressure, but catch rates dropped to around two fish per day in the late 1940s.

Since that time, fishing on the lake appears to have been cyclical, with several years of good fishing and large fish, alternating with periods of reduced abundance.

Lake Whitefish. Whitefish are high in food value, were undoubtedly used as a food fish by Native Americans and were important commercially until about 1900. When caught, they were either frozen, pickled in salt, or smoked and stored in barrels, and sold in southern Maine fish markets and throughout New England. They were enjoyed as a winter food supplement at logging camps. Rural families also made annual trips to lakes to net, snare, or spear whitefish as they ascended tributaries in dense numbers to spawn during November. Whitefish could be taken by gill net during the summer, but the use of gill nets in all Maine waters was made unlawful in 1955.

The overall color of a whitefish is silvery dark brown with black or black-tipped fins, and the scales are large. They were said to be good fighters and were commonly 14" – 20 " in length and weighed 1-3 lbs.

An account of whitefish given in the 1867 Report of the Commissioners of Inland Fisheries and Game, provides excellent

Fishing and Hunting Resources

insight into the early fisheries for this species, its habits, and sporting qualities:

> "In the Fish River region, in Moosehead Lake, in Schoodic Grand, they pronounce the whitefish the best of the fishes .... In Moosehead Lake they sometimes take a fly. In June last we saw one taken with the fly near Mt. Kineo ... It weighed a pound and a half ... They can be taken with the hook at any season of the year in deep water. Almost any bait will answer, but the best is a piece of a small fish."[13]

In a 1961 Maine Fish and Game Department article titled "Whitefish – Are Anglers Missing a Bet?" fishery biologist Owen Fenderson wrote of the qualities of the species, which was often overlooked by trout and salmon anglers at the time. A resurgence of the lake whitefish sport fishery began developing around the early 1970s, and a species that was considered an "almost game fish" grew into a highly sought-after species, particularly by winter anglers. The widespread use of snowmobiles made many waters more accessible to ice fishermen. Since jigging through the ice is a very effective way to catch whitefish, the species became a significant part of the wintertime catch.

A 2016 report available at (maine.gov › docs › fisheries-reports "Current Status of Whitefish in Maine") concluded, however, that:

> "... lake whitefish declines have coincided with the introduction of rainbow smelt. A current research project within the Maine Department of Fisheries and Wildlife is attempting to better understand the exact mechanisms that are driving the whitefish-smelt interaction, and find ways to mitigate the problems and inform whitefish recovery efforts.
>
> Restrictive fishing regulations over the past two decades, and a whitefish hatchery stocking program (from 2003-2009) appear to have helped in some waters, but have resulted in

limited success to date. Recently we have seen very positive results in waters with increased numbers of lake trout, which have caused depressed smelt numbers. These low smelt numbers appear to have reduced the level of smelt-whitefish interaction and resulted in encouraging levels of whitefish reproduction."

Salmon. Landlocked salmon are not native to Moosehead Lake. About 1875 or 1876, they were introduced into its waters by the state Fish and Game Commissioner and Orrin Dennis of Kineo. Since then, the salmon have increased so rapidly that Moosehead has become one of the best salmon waters in New England.

Historically, one of the most popular ways of fishing for landlocked salmon was with a fly rod, either on a lake or a river. Many river waters are restricted to fly fishing only using artificial lures such as streamers, bucktails, wet flies, nymphs, and dry flies. On lakes, either long shanked or tandem trolling flies, or sewn smelts, are traditional Maine tactics. Stream, river, and lake fishing for landlocked salmon is usually best from mid-April through the months of May and June over much of the state, and into mid-July in a select few spots. After that, action tapers off until September when crisp nights and fall rains cool water temperatures, and salmon start to prepare for their spawning run.

Squaretailed Trout. Although not as large as togue or salmon, some are three pounds in size. A fine-tasting, scrappy fish, they can be found in the shallows during the summer. Not to be confused with brook trout, in Moosehead Lake these trout have been found to spawn in the lake itself. Open water fishing is best in May and June, and ice fishing in shallow water is also usually productive.

Brook Trout. Also known as squaretails, the size of eastern brook trout varies greatly, depending on water temperature, productivity, and food sources. The statewide average length of three-year-old brook trout in Maine lakes is 13.3". Stream populations are typically slower growing than lake populations. Some high elevation trout populations mature and reproduce at lengths smaller than 6". Brook trout prefer cold water between 50 and 65 degrees and thrive in clear, clean, well-oxygenated waters, although populations are heavily influenced by their environment.

Color is variable, depending on habitat. Brook trout can be distinguished from other members of the trout family by the red spots with blue halos, and yellow and pink spots on their sides, a dark, wavy line on their back, and the white leading edges of their fins and tail.

In the spring and fall, brook trout can be caught near shore or on the surface using small dry flies, streamers, copper lures, and worms. During the summer months, they're more likely to be found in depths of 10' to 35', and can be caught using spin casting, fly fishing, or trolling rods and reels.

Brook trout are fun to catch by ice fishing as well. During winter months, they are found close to shore in water depths of 4' to 12' using minnows, worms, or copper jigs.

Togue (Lake Trout). Lake trout have a typical trout-shaped body covered with creamy white spots on a background of bronze, dark brown, or green. Their coloration can resemble brook trout but lack the colorful spots of a brook trout. Another distinguishing feature of lake trout is a deeply forked tail as opposed to the square tail of the brook trout.

In most waters, lake trout commonly reach lengths of 18" to 24" and weights of 2 to 4 lbs. They are among the longest lived and largest freshwater game fish, often living 20 years or more and attaining sizes of over 30" and 10 lbs.

Lake trout are voracious and adaptable feeders, foraging on a wide variety of aquatic organisms, from plankton to crayfish to smelts to white perch. They are deep dwellers that prefer very cold water year-round. In the spring and fall, lake trout can be caught close to shore by casting or trolling using streamer flies, minnows, or lures.

In the summer, the best method of fishing for them is trolling with lead core line or downriggers using minnows or copper, white, or silver lures. In late June, July, and August, they are typically caught at depths below 45'.

Ice fishing for lake trout can be quite productive in water depths between 10' and 100', using smelt, shiners, and suckers, or silver, white, or copper jigs.

Smallmouth Bass. Smallmouth bass were introduced illegally to the lake in recent years but are now well-established in Spencer Bay and Lily Bay. In fact, Moosehead Lake was listed No. 72 in the Top 100 Bass Lakes by Bassmaster in 2014. Biologists believe the smallmouth bass are a detriment to the salmonids in the fishery, and the state Department of Inland Fisheries and Wildlife now issues permits for catch-and-kill tournaments.

Big Game. Maine's surface area is 82% forested and is unique among eastern states for this relatively undeveloped landscape. The northern hardwood and coniferous forests are distributed statewide and comprise 40% of Maine's landscape. Vegetation and snowfall patterns in northern Maine are most conducive to wildlife adapted to areas with severe winters (including moose and bear), while southern and coastal portions of the state have much milder winters that are more hospitable for deer and wild turkey.

Hunting seasons for **moose, deer, and bear** are in the fall, and in 1893 the per-hunter bag limits were one moose, two caribou, and three deer.

Before 1899, **caribou** were one of the state's most important big game animals, attracting "sports" from all over the country, but it has been illegal to hunt caribou in Maine since then. Reports persisted of a small herd in the Katahdin region until 1914. Efforts to reintroduce small herds of caribou into Maine were undertaken in 1963 and again in 1993, but both of these reintroduction programs failed.

The Bangor and Aroostook Railroad, which provided flatcar service in northern Maine for transporting game animals shot by sportsmen, recorded the number of animal carcasses moved each year by flatcar. Greenville station statistics are not always mentioned, but the following chart shows the arc of big game shot by sports and transported between 1895 and 1924.

Big Game Shipped from Greenville Via the Bangor and Aroostook Railroad

Year	Deer	Moose	Bear
1895	1581	112	N/A
1900	3379	210	N/A
1905	4623	207	38
1910	4606	93	13
1915	2596	104	41
1920	2518	119	20
1924	1661	N/A	26

Management of Maine's big game species requires the ongoing collection of biological data to monitor populations, as well as information from harvested animals and hunters (surveys and licensing data). Mandatory registration of harvested animals provides critical information including the sex, age, location, method, timing of harvest, and other biological data. These data are used to calculate hunter success rates and inform biological data sets.

Fishing and Hunting Resources

The Maine Department of Inland Fisheries and Wildlife (MDIFW) has long partnered with private businesses to register most harvested deer, moose, turkey, and bear. These registration agents attach a seal to each animal and record pertinent information on paper forms for submission to the department. Information from the forms is then entered into a database for biologists' use. Although this system has worked well for many years, technology has now made it possible to record this data more efficiently and accurately.

Bird Hunting. Bird hunting is not frequently mentioned in most sporting camp literature, but fall hunting seasons are open for woodcock, ruffed grouse (partridge), and turkeys. Duck species hunted are mergansers, black ducks, mallards, and wild geese.

In the Maine Woods (1924, p 70) the annual B&A Railroad hunting and fishing publication, had this to say about hunting partridge (grouse) and woodcock:

> "**Partridge** are comparatively tame and fly 75' to 90' a second. This means they provide sport for the hunter who uses a rifle instead of a shotgun. Partridge shooting with a rifle is something entirely apart from using the shotgun, and calls for the most skilled marksmanship. The sport comes in shooting the partridge in the head which makes a clean hit, which means that the bird's body is unharmed. For the woman who wants to try her skill with the rifle, there is no better test than partridge hunting with a 22-caliber rifle, and the woman who can "crown" a partridge is entitled to a badge of merit. In alertness and sagacity, a partridge is unsurpassed, and to bring down a partridge requires quickness, sureness, and agility of decision. Then it is a matter of less than seconds to swing the gun to the shoulder, unlock the safety, and pull the trigger.
>
> In the daytime, **woodcock** drowse in the fields and open stretches. When it is come upon by the dog, it is slow to shake

off its napping. It is in this drowsy stage that hunters get their point and prize. Woodcock hunting is a premier form of sport in the Maine woods. The woodcock is the same bird that is known variously in the southern states as the brier-snipe, the swamp snipe, and the ghost bird. ... The best season for woodcock shooting is from the 10th to the 25th of October. In the fall, woodcock follow the valleys of streams and rivers in their line of flight and reach the coast by following the rivers to sea and thence onto their migration to the equatorial region."

Guides

Since the mid-1800s, the state of Maine has produced the unique occupational specialty of the Maine guide. Renowned as an expert woodsman, the Maine guide took clients or "sports" into the deep woods, onto lake waters, or to follow streams in search of quarry and adventure. The guide served both as adviser and servant; they showed clients to areas where fish, deer, and bear could be found, suggested methods that would lead to a successful hunt. They packed and unpacked canoes, prepared camp, cooked meals, fixed equipment, pitched tents, and paddled or poled the canoe into the wilderness. The guide was a unique regional adaptation to the rising national interest in hunting, fishing, and outdoor life in the late nineteenth century, and became an institution in the northern woods and a key component of interior Maine's tourist industry.

Farrar's 1884 *Illustrated Guide to Moosehead Lake, North Wood Wilderness* reported that at the Kineo Pier, the guides with their birch skiffs are on the lake:

> "At 9:00 a.m. or earlier, often with wives or daughters accompanying the fishermen and go to the famous fishing-pools returning at night with the brilliantly spotted game, which is served at breakfast the following morning. The guides have wonderful skill in handling these birches [canoes] in quick water and amidst heavy seas. They are Yankees, Indians, and half-breeds, intelligent, thoroughly wide-awake and interested in all that relates to backwoods life, and capable of storytelling to any extent.
>
> At the Mt. Kineo House one can obtain the best of guides. They are practical woodsmen, good natured, tough, and hardy, and use their best endeavors to please you. They can tell you about fishing, hunting, and show you any place you may wish to visit. ... Their terms are $3 per day while about

the hotel, and on trips $3 plus board. They furnish canoe, tent, and cooking utensils; the party engaging them supplies the provisions."

To set standards for the guide's professional performance, in 1897 each guide was required by law to register with the state fish and game commissioners and procure a certificate "setting forth that he is deemed suitable to act as a guide." In 1897, on a statewide basis, 1,316 guides became registered, and 1,760 men and three women registered in 1898 as professional guides. The law limited a guide to having no more than five clients at one time.

Two years later, the State Legislature passed a law requiring nonresident hunters and fishermen to hire guides during certain seasons. The bill was supported by the Inland Fish and Game Commission, the guides themselves, and a powerful lobby of lumbermen and timberland owners who feared that unsupervised sporting activity posed a fire danger in the forestlands.

By 1920, the northern Maine guiding community was at its peak. Not surprisingly, guiding could be divided into guide and client perspectives about their relationships: 1) the guide thought they were most important and 2) the client thought they were most important. In the guide's mind, their first responsibility was to look after the client's welfare, follow safety precautions, cook good meals, and make sure that the client had a good time. In the client's mind, however, the guide was hired primarily to locate fish and game. Certainly, many of the sportsmen were good outdoorsmen, but others were inexperienced and had to be watched closely.

In addition to guarding the safety of the client, the guide was obliged to see that they were comfortable. It was important to the guide that his charges have proper clothes, boots, and equipment. Poorly equipped clients would be unhappy, and this would affect the guide's chance of being rehired the following season.

The guide's role in support of a client on a fishing or hunting trip at a remote location began early in the morning. The guide would begin by building fires in the cabins or at camping sites. As the guests dressed and ate breakfast, the guide readied the canoe with paddles, poles, seats, cushions, hunting or fishing gear, and the cooking equipment for lunch. Before leaving, he would confer with the other guides to ensure that each of the sporting parties would have peace and solitude on their journey.

Around noontime, whether the client had bagged a prize or not, the guide would begin to cook lunch, a tradition known as "dinnering out." The guide's cooking kit usually consisted of a cast-iron fry pan, a tin coffee pot, a set of metal "agate" dishes, and some silverware. Over an open fire or two, the guide would pan-fry or broil fresh game or fish. The most common fare was trout fried in pork fat with strips of bacon placed inside. In addition, the guide might cook pancakes, johnnycake, toast, or vegetables, and brew tea or strong coffee. The real cooking challenge for the guides was the meal that had to be cooked in a reflector oven. This device captured heat from the fire to bake pies and biscuits, and baking items evenly with a reflector oven often taxed the cooking skills of the guide.

After lunch, guide and sport would continue the hunt. At the end of a long day, they would return to camp and the comfort of a warm fire, and likely consume a few alcoholic beverages. Here, around a campfire or fireplace, the guide had a repertoire of stories to tell about his experiences in the woods. The client would reciprocate with a tale of their own from the city; in this exchange, a friendship would often develop that kept the client returning to the same guide year after year."

MAINE'S GUIDES

THE game and forest laws of Maine are justly very strict. Non-residents of the state may not enter upon the wild lands of the state and camp or kindle fires thereon while engaged in hunting or fishing without being in charge of a registered guide during the months of May, June, July, August, September, October and November, and no registered guide shall, at the same time, guide or be employed by more than five non-residents in hunting.

It is not necessary for a non-resident to employ a guide provided he is stopping with the owner of a registered camp, and does not camp and kindle fires while hunting or fishing.

The Maine guide, who charges $3 a day (sometimes less) and his board, is the best fellow in the world; it is both pleasant and profitable to share a canoe or tent with him.

> "It is different in the Old World, where people are frightfully apprehensive of losing caste by hobnobbing with their servants and huntsmen. The guides of the north woods are in almost all cases as much companions as servants. They keep their places and are respectful, but they are, with few exceptions, men of a certain independence of character and know their own worth; The man who is afraid of losing dignity by helping his guide in the duties of camp life would be a ridiculous, not to say contemptible figure on this side of the Atlantic."—("The Way of the Woods.")

Most guides are adepts with pack, paddle and pole, and know the country and the fishing art intimately, as well as deer-hunting; but if the sportsman is after moose, it is better to engage some well-known man beforehand.

Guides

CAMP AT HEAD OF LAKE. [From *Harper's Magazine*.

Two guides will prepare a meal while the three sports await. Farrar's *Moosehead Lake, North Woods Wilderness*, 1884.

Guides

Dr. Everett Parker, in his book *Kineo, Moosehead sentinel from Native Americans to hotel grandeur*, lists the names of 142 men who were identified as "Licensed Guides of Kineo" in the early 1900s. From that number, it's clear that there were a significant number of guides employed by the sporting camp industry.

After World War II, however, social change and technological advances undermined the role of the guide. By the 1950s, guests began bringing their own boats and fishing or hunting gear, staying in housekeeping cabins rather than at a sporting camp, and hiring a guide for a day or longer.[14]

Parker, in *The Moosehead Lake Region 1900-1950*, included this photo of guides employed at the Mt. Kineo Hotel in 1912.

Scores of men from Greenville and Rockwood were employed by the Mount Kineo Hotel to guide visitors on hunting and fishing expeditions. This photograph shows a group of guides in 1912. Among the men pictured here are Bill Meservey, Joe Murray, Amos Thibodeau, Angus Miller, Simon Mayhew, Edgar Harlow, John Mansell, Louis Nicholas, Blackhawk Palmer, Joe Gero, Louis Bernard, Peter Plourde, George Leith, Jim Duff, John Fecto, Roy Nelson, Peter Tomer, Bill Moriarty, Henry Johnson, Oscar Mitchell, Ernest Ham, Frank Tomer, Al Cripps, and Newell Francis.

Guides

Guides and their sports, *In the Maine Woods,* 1909.

Among the most famous of Maine guides was Chief Henry Red Eagle Perley.

facebook.com, Facebook Groups.
This group is dedicated to the study of Henry Perley, AKA Chief Henry Red Eagle, a Greenville native son, silent movie actor, and writer.

Guides

One of Moosehead Lake's most famous guides was Henry Perley (1885–1972). Of Malecite Indian descent, he was an actor, entertainer, wilderness guide, and author. Commonly known by his pseudonym, Chief Henry Red Eagle, Perley became the youngest licensed guide in the state of Maine at age 14. He attended Greenville High School, and was the first full-blooded Indian to graduate from there; he was also class president and graduated valedictorian of his class in 1902.

Perley made his first appearance in traveling shows with the Kickapoo Indian Medicine Show in the United States, where he performed in full tribal regalia. He later joined Buffalo Bill's Wild West Show and the Barnum and Bailey Circus. Perley often played the role of Indians stereotyped as savages during the early 1900s.

He appeared in numerous silent films with actors and actresses such as Mary Pickford, the Gish Sisters, Rudolph Valentino, and Richard Dix.

Perley began his writing career under the pseudonym "Henry Red Eagle" in 1910, writing short stories for pulp magazines such as Argosy, Top-Notch Stories, Open Road for Boys, and All-Story Weekly. In the 1930s, Perley moved back to the Moosehead Lake Region, where he worked as a wilderness guide, camp caretaker, and electrician. He became well-established as a renowned storyteller who advocated for environmental conservation. Perley's stories encompassed themes of lumbering and adventures of wilderness guides. Focusing on New England, he often highlighted the indigenous peoples' presence there to counteract the common understanding that they had disappeared from the northeastern United States. Wikipedia

Guides

> *"His writings were more than just melodrama or a simple record of canoeing and camping practices. They were part of a complex dialogue between Native American culture, white fascination with the primitive, and the industrial use of the forest. Red Eagle worked within the stylistic and thematic parameters of this literature, while offering critiques — sometimes humorous, sometimes indignant — of the impact of modernity on the Maine north woods. By referencing his own Native American consciousness, he could insert this critical commentary in his pro-tourist and pro-industry writing and still pay tribute to the themes that defined this literature: native uses of the forest and the never-ending expansion of Maine woods tourism. His writings spanned a thirty-year period of enormous change in the Maine woods and in public ideas about the Maine woods. His ideas reflected these changes, but they also expressed the unique perspectives of a man committed to two worlds and living within the wilderness environment he described so effectively and so personally."* (Potts, Dale, Maine History magazine, Vol.43, Number 2, p. 212, Raymond H. Fogler Library, DigitalCommons@UMaine)
>
> Chief Henry Red Eagle died in Greenville in 1972.

In 1997, twenty-five years after Perley's death, his niece and granddaughter published a volume of some of his writings titled *Aboriginally Yours*

Leased Land

For some of the sporting camps described in this book, it's noted that they were, or are, located on leased land. Before 1899, timberlands with lake frontage were primarily owned by individuals who sold stumpage (rights to harvest trees) and by lumbermen who bought the land and logged it. After 1900, lumber companies and paper mills themselves acquired ownership of forest lands to secure their source of supply.

Companies such as Hollingsworth and Whitney (H&W), the J.M. Huber Lumber Corporation, Scott Paper Company, and Prentiss & Carlisle proactively leased lots for camp and cottage development on lakefront and riverfront lands.

For the corporations, reasons for leasing shorefront included: 1) generating corporate goodwill because individuals could build sporting camps or cottages under a long-term lease arrangement requiring annual lease payments, and 2) gaining some investment return from areas on which timber harvesting was otherwise prohibited by shoreland development restrictions.

The advantage for the leasees was avoiding the cost of the outright purchase of waterfront land, which most could not have afforded.

Some timberland corporations have changed their leasing policies over the years, and either no longer offer leases or require leaseholders to purchase the land on which their camps have been constructed if they want to keep them. New leases are rarely created, but existing leases are sometimes transferrable to a new owner.

Forestland Conservation

One of the remarkable aspects of Maine's northern forests is that although they're privately owned, they are, by and large, open for public recreation. Additionally, the vast road networks of paper companies and those who harvest timber for construction of homes and other structures, allow the public to drive their vehicles on these roads for access to campgrounds, individual camps, hunting and fishing sites, and for other forms of recreation. Large landowners often adopt land use rules and regulations, usually based on state law, to prevent erosion and the fouling of streams by ATVs and other vehicles, thus respecting the woodlands to keep them as productive "working forests." In recent years, the trend for using conservation easements to place limitations on future land development to preserve working forestlands has expanded significantly.

With only 6% of Maine land being publicly owned, access ultimately depends on the willingness of private landowners to allow hunting and other outdoor activities on their properties. Maine has a unique tradition of "implied access," which means that unless signs are posted prohibiting access, the public can legally access private land. With the exception of some large industrial landowners that charge road-use and/or camping fees, access to private land is free. The open land tradition of private landowners allowing hunting on their properties may be slowly changing, as surveys conducted of small landowners have documented a dramatic increase in the amount of posted land. A number of factors may be at play, including increases in motorized All-Terrain Vehicles (ATVs), demographic shifts by landowners, and changing cultural attitudes towards hunting. These trends apply to small landowners but are also evidenced by changes in ownership of large parcels in northern Maine that have also resulted in some loss in access for hunters.[15]

Forestland Conservation

Forest Society of Maine. Around Moosehead Lake, hundreds of thousands of acres of working forest have been placed under conservation easements for which compliance is monitored by the Forest Society of Maine (FSM). FSM is a state-wide land trust particularly focused on Maine's north woods, the largest expanse of forestland east of the Rocky Mountains.

FSM has helped pioneer landscape-scale forestland conservation through the development and implementation of conservation easements to sustain the ecological, economic, cultural, and recreational values of Maine's forests. Since its founding in 1984, FSM has helped conserve more than one million acres of forestland. It strives to encourage thoughtful dialogue and conservation actions that encompass the full array of interests and ownerships in Maine's north woods.

FSM is supported by donations from businesses and people who care about the future of this great forest of 12 million acres of productive forestland, with its 5,000 lakes, its more than 4,000 acres of canoeable rivers and streams, and its abundance and diversity of wildlife. The goal is to have this great and unique forest endure.

North Maine Woods, Inc. (NMW) was created in 1971 by the private family and industrial landowners in the NMW region. NMW was formed as a not-for-profit organization to manage public access for hunting, fishing, camping, and recreation, so the forest landowners could concentrate on managing their forest products. Although NMW charges recreational user fees at NMW gates, under its non-profit status none of the receipts can be shared with the landowner members. Despite increases in the numbers of visitors, the management program now in place allows landowners to move harvesting crews and equipment, and truck harvested wood from the region, in a safe manner.

Forestland Conservation

With many different landowners in the program and each with their own forest management style, the result is a very diverse management of northern Maine forest resources. Some owners conduct intensive harvest and regeneration programs, and some have created significant ecological reserve areas where no harvesting or road building is allowed. And then there are many owners that manage their forests somewhere in the middle of the spectrum.

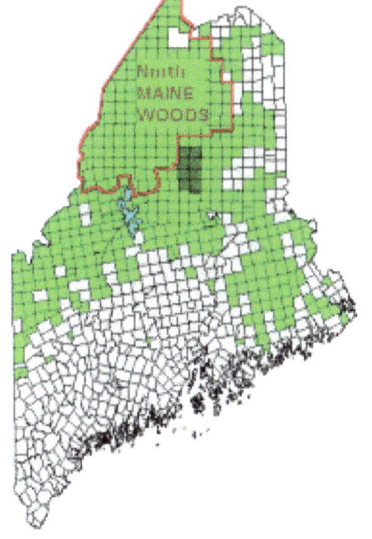

About 30% of the total NMW area of 3.5 million acres is included in conservation easements which protect various aspects of the forest.

The state of Maine has negotiated a large conservation easement around Moosehead Lake, particularly around the more undeveloped north bay, to offset development rights approved for the southern part of the lake. Nine miles of Moosehead Lake shoreline are under state conservation easements there.

NMW operational area, the dark green is Baxter State Park.maineanencyclopedia.com/maine-north-woods.

The state owns outright the 980-acre Farm Island near Mt. Kineo that was gifted by Julia E. Crafts Sheridan and R. Philip Sheridan in 1971, the 935-acre Lily Bay State Park gifted by Scott Paper Company in 1961, the 4,208-acre Sugar Island purchased from Scott Paper Company by the state of Maine in 1985, and 800 acres of the northerly portion of the Mt. Kineo peninsula that was purchased as a state park in 1990.

Watercraft, Snowmobiles, ATVs, and Mountain Bikes

The invention and development of mechanical technologies to expand recreational opportunities and outdoor adventures for individuals, families, and groups with similar interests has continued over the decades. Consequently, the type and character of sporting camp clientele has evolved and will continue to do so.

Watercraft. Boats powered by both inboard and outboard engines are prime users of Moosehead Lake waters for fishing, touring, exploring, water skiing, and tubing. For boats brought to the lake by trailer, there are state owned launch facilities at four locations on the east shore: Lily Bay State Park, Jewett Cove, Cowan Cove, and Norcross Brook. On the west shore, launch ramps are at Greenville Junction and Rockwood. Marinas are located on the Moose River, at The Birches Resort, at Greenville, and at Beaver Cove, and provide dockage and winter storage for larger inboard-powered craft. Canoes, kayaks, stand-up paddleboards, personal watercraft, outboard and inboard monohulls, and pontoon boats can be rented at many sporting camps and at marinas.

Snowmobiles. Northern Maine receives abundant snowfall, and the Moosehead Lake region usually gets over 100" of snowfall each year, making this area a destination for snowmobilers.

Maine's snowmobile trail system, which includes 4,000 miles of primary trail known as the Interconnected Trail System (ITS), offers the opportunity to ride uninterrupted from region to region, with a full range of services available along various routes. The Moosehead Loop Trail, on which one can ride anywhere from 138 to 166 miles depending on the route taken, is Maine's longest snowmobile loop trail. There are more than 280 snowmobile clubs in Maine, and many of the state's 10,000 miles of non-ITS trails are groomed by local snowmobile clubs. (For a map of Maine's ITS and trail conditions reports, visit the Maine Snowmobile Association's website.)

Many outfitters, sporting camps, and resorts offer complete snowmobile rentals, from helmets and "sleds" to services and fuel. One can also take advantage of guided sled tours, ranging from half- and full-day outings for families and groups to extended trips of a few days or more.

All-Terrain Vehicles (ATVs). The Moosehead Lake area's local ATV trail volunteers undertake responsibility for maintaining well-marked trails throughout the region. Trails from Greenville reach The Forks on the Kennebec River, Rockwood, Kokadjo, and Northeast Carry. The opportunities for adventures are truly endless with ponds and mountains to explore and wildlife to watch. The trail systems make it possible to go out for just a couple hours of fun or make it a full day expedition. ATVs can be rented at sporting camps or from local businesses. Setting up a guided ATV trip can often give the best riding experience.

Many ATV trails are on private land, and riders are requested to ride safely and respect the property of landowners who generously permit trail use by the public. Greenville and Rockwood allow ATVs to travel on certain municipal roads giving riders the ability to access restaurants and shops; signs direct where and when ATVs are permitted to travel on roads.

Mountain Biking. The popularity of mountain biking is growing quickly in the Moosehead Lake region. The newly formed Moosehead Outdoor Trail Alliance is also a member of the New England Mountain Bike Association (NEMBA) and is interfacing with businesses, sporting camps, and the State Bureau of Parks and Recreation to develop a trail network.

Sporting Camps Today and Tomorrow

Author Alice Arlen, in her book *Maine Sporting Camps*, describes the appeal of sporting camps in today's world as follows: "The essence of the sporting-camp experience is a deep sense of permanence, continuity, and connectedness. Strangers share their hearts' desires around tables or campfires, generations sing songs under brilliant stars or around the camp piano. ... At a time when it is easier to find virtual electronic stimulus, and increasingly difficult finding places where one can truly reconnect with human rhythms, we can all count ourselves fortunate that a small group of hard-working, individualistic men and women have kept sporting-camp traditions alive."[16]

Because sporting camps are surrounded by woods and waters that endure as working forestlands, the Moosehead Lake region and Maine's north woods offer rich potential for continuation of the sporting camp hunting and fishing traditions, modified, of course, by evolving watercraft, snowmobile, and ATV options, and by communications technology, trends in hiking, and increased opportunities for other outdoor recreational pursuits. The expanded use of conservation easements by these private timberland landowners, with the easements being held and monitored by entities such as the Forest Society of Maine, will provide certainty of public access to waters and woodlands for the future.

The non-profit Maine Sporting Camp Heritage Foundation was founded to help secure the future of sporting camps, and its purposes and functions are described in this information on their website:

The Maine Sporting Camp Heritage Foundation
The Maine Sporting Camp Heritage Foundation was founded to preserve Maine's traditional sporting camps and the natural resources they rely

upon. The Foundation's core mission is to preserve this part of Maine's cultural heritage so that future generations will continue to have access to some of Maine's most wild and scenic locations and will be able to enjoy the outdoor experiences that sporting camps offer.

An important outcome of preserving the "Maine Sporting Camp Experience" is the preservation and strengthening of the local economies that depend on the continued operation of one or more traditional sporting camps. In addition, further economic deterioration, and increased unemployment in the communities whose economies depend to a large extent on visitors to these traditional Maine sporting camps, will be limited.

PRESERVING TRADITIONS

In 1904, there were at least 300 sporting camps in operation in Maine. By 2007, this number had dwindled to fewer than 40. As more commercial camps are lost, this unique part of Maine's cultural heritage comes dangerously close to losing its critical mass and disappearing altogether — taking with it the vital role these sporting camps play in Maine's overall economy and its tradition of outdoor recreation.

The "Sporting Camp Experience" is as unique today as it was 150 years ago. These family-run businesses offer rustic cabins surrounded by spectacular wild scenery and abundant wildlife; the lost art of providing hearty home-cooked meals and pastries; safe family vacation settings; and traditional outdoor recreation like fishing, hunting, hiking and wildlife watching.

The Foundation's educational programs enable the public to learn about traditional Maine sporting camps, the vital role they play in Maine's cultural heritage, economic well-being, and the importance of conservation efforts to preserve Maine's natural resources and the undeveloped, pristine surroundings that sporting camps rely upon.

The Foundation provides training and technical assistance to sporting camp owners and operators that helps them better manage their operations and market their camps in an economic environment where it appears that interest in traditional sporting camp activities such as fishing and hunting are waning. Working with our partner organizations, assistance topics range from general business, marketing and advertising, and new product and service offerings, to business planning and budgeting the Foundation is also able to offer affordable financing to sporting camps for such purposes as:

- Upgrading camp facilities in order to make them more suitable for today's visitors.

Sporting Camps Today and Tomorrow

- Assisting in the acquisition of the underlying land for sporting camps located on leased property, in the event the landowner elects to offer the property for sale.
- Directly acquiring property in the event it is offered for sale by the landowner, and then lease it to a camp operator in order to assure that the sporting camp is preserved and public access is maintained.

RESTORING PUBLIC ACCESS

Maine Sporting Camps face serious challenges to their survival. Changes in land ownership and land management policies, high land valuations and taxes, lack of long-term land leases, increased government regulation, lack of affordable capital, and encroaching development all threaten the future of Maine's remaining sporting camps.

Most sporting camps are located on waterfront land that typically can be sold at prices far higher than what could be supported by a commercial sporting camp operation. Many camps have already been purchased by individuals and families, who then convert the camps into exclusive-use, private vacation properties - the end result is loss of public access to Maine's wildlands. By preserving the sporting camps and the natural resources they rely upon, the Foundation will prevent that loss of access.

Our ability to offer affordable financing to sporting camps for a limited range of purposes helps ensure that the Maine sporting camp is preserved and public access to Maine's natural resources and wildlife is maintained.

HABITAT CONSERVATION

Maine's Sporting Camps were established 100 to 150 years ago in locations then surrounded by miles and miles of forest and wetland habitat. "Development" was absent, rare plants were undisturbed, and wildlife like deer, moose, caribou, lynx, black bear, pine marten, eagles, salmon, and brook trout were plentiful. The natural habitat that provided for wildlife also made it possible for sporting camps to sustain their existence as attractive places for outdoor recreation and enrichment.

Today, Maine Sporting Camps and their surrounding habitats face serious challenges. Changes in land ownership and land management policies, high land valuations and taxes, and encroaching development all threaten the future of Maine's remaining Sporting Camps.

The Foundation maintains a database of every commercially active sporting camp, plus those that have already been converted to private, non-public use. We survey the outstanding wildlife, habitats, ecosystems, and scenic values nearby. The Foundation then builds coalitions to establish conservation easements in order to protect the undeveloped, pristine surroundings and

Sporting Camps Today and Tomorrow

wildlife habitats that make sporting camps such special places and provide for the public's need for remote outdoor recreation.

MAINE SPORTING CAMP HERITAGE FOUNDATION · PO BOX 136 · HAMPDEN, MAINE 04444.

Index to Camp Locations

Camps at North Bay

Northeast Carry		Seboomook		West Shore
#1 Penobscot Inn & Trading Post	#4	Northwest Carry Inn/	#6	Camps Caribou/ Whileaway/ Ogontz
#2 Northeast Carry Inn/ Winnegarnock House & Trading Post	#5	Seboomook House/ Seboomook Campground		
#3 Raymond's Country Store & Cabins				

Camps from Rockwood to Spencer Pond

West Shore		East Shore/Spencer Bay	Kokadjo
#7 Tomhegan Camps	#13	Mt. Kineo Resort	#17 Kokadjo Inn & Camps
#8 The Birches	#14	Folsom Farm	#18 Kokadjo Cabins & Trading Post
#9 Maynard's in Maine	#15	Spencer Pond Camps	
#10 Gray Ghost Camps	#16	Spencer Bay Camps	#19 Northern Pride Lodge
#11 Whitten's Inn, Camps & Cottages			#20 Roach River House
#12 West Outlet Camps/ Gilbert & Coombs/ Old Mill Campground			#21 Second Roach Pond Camps/Medawisla
			#22 Randall's/Chadwick's/ West Branch Pond

Camps at South Bay

West Shore and Deer Island		Sugar Island	Lily Bay, Beaver Cove & Sandy Bay
#23 Marr's Indian Pond Camps	#28	Thorofare Camps/ Moosehead Camps/ Wilderness Camps/ Eagle Haven Camp	#31 Wheat's Island Camps
#24 Wilson's East Outlet Camps			#32 Lily Bay House
#25 Moose (Squaw) Mountain Inn & Cabins			#33 Beaver Cove Camps
#26 Miller's Training Camps	#29	Camp Greenleaf/ Sugar Island Camp	#34 Whitten's Lodge & Camps
#27 The Capen's	#30	Porcupine Camps	#35 Camp Allagash/ Crow's Nest

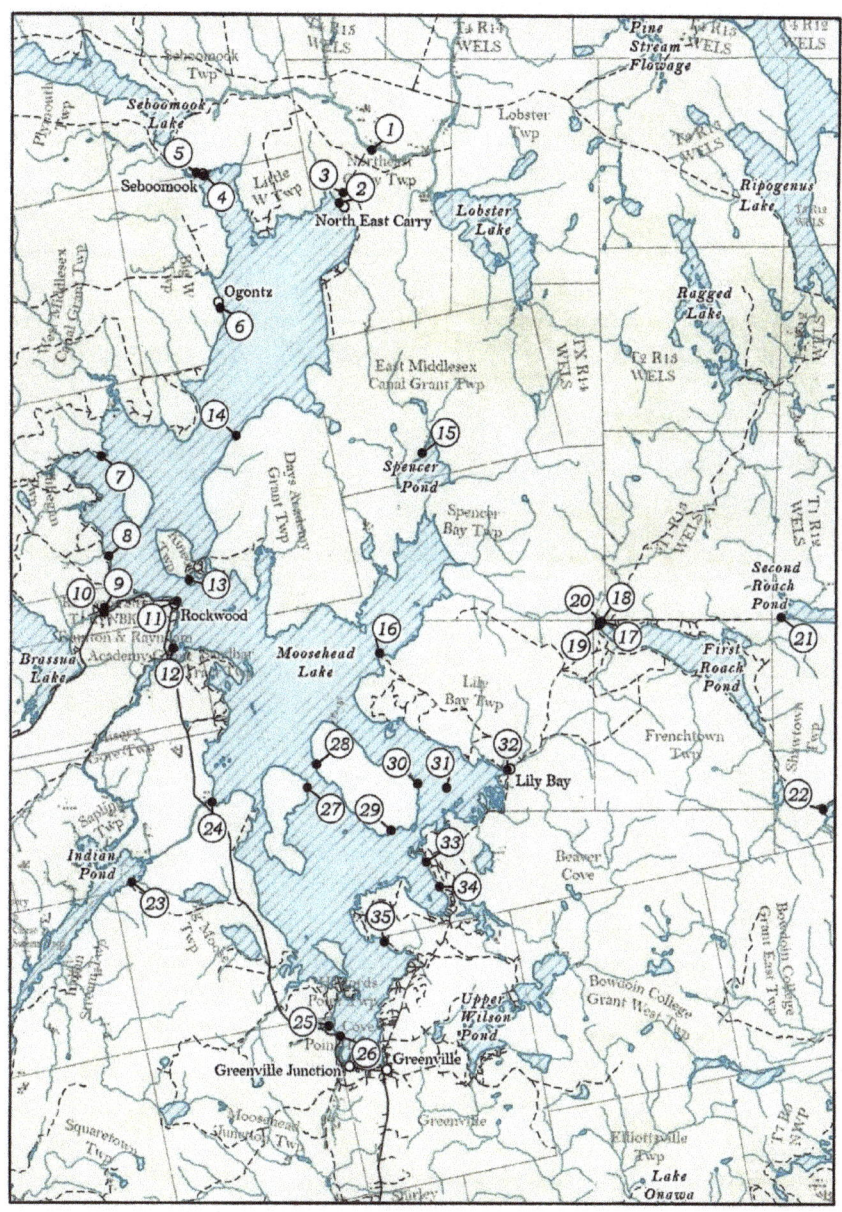

Map prepared by Carl Morrison, Winslow, Maine, in ArcGIS Pro from spatial data provided by the Maine GeoLibrary, ESRI and its data partners, USGS and the GIS User Community.

Camp Allagash - The Crow's Nest

Sandy Bay on Moosehead Lake's east shore is a Salmon Run of the Scammon property, because Bigney's mother, Lydia, had married Benjamin Scammon. The first building on the site was a three-story log cabin named "The Crow's Nest" by Capt. Fred Bigney's wife Henrietta Rowe. Bigney added a lodge and served sportsmen and sportswomen as clientele.

In the Maine Woods ad, 1901.

Ads promised splendid views, lots of peace and quiet, fishing, swimming, boating, and prime hunting. "Better Location - Better Beds and Table – Better Treatment, Your Enjoyment - Our Policy."

The Crow's Nest sporting camp was closed about 1917 when it was sold to Gordon "Ike" Saunders and John Brown who rented the camp's 50 acres and leased another 150 acres. Saunders and Brown turned it into a boys' camp named Camp Allagash. A highlight of the camp's summer program was taking campers on extended canoe trips to the Allagash and St. John Rivers. Saunder's wife Edna Mae worked at the Haverford School, which still operates as a private boys' school on Philadelphia's Main Line. Haverford School 7th grade teacher, athletic director, and licensed Maine guide Arthur W. Palmer, and Fred "Doc" Wallace, served as the Camp Allagash directors from when it opened in 1917 until 1934. Most of the staff

Camp Allagash – The Crow's Nest

and campers were drawn from private schools attended by Philadelphia Main Line families.

The Crow's Nest postcard. Bowdoin.edu/ History/ES 247 Reading Guide.

As with some other lakeside camps, Camp Allagash was historically accessible only via the lake, and several small steamers operated to transport clients and guests to the camps. The Bigneys operated their own small steamer, and vessels owned by the camp during the Palmer years were *Pea Kay*, *Silver Spray*, and *Edna Mae*. Later owners used the small steamer *Sprite*.

In 1947, Fred Bigney's daughter Henrietta sold the 50-acre camp site to Arthur W. Palmer, Sr., and R. Frank Brattan; Brattan later deeded his ownership in the property to Palmer who died in 1948. The summer camp for boys was then run by his daughter Jane Palmer Barr and her husband George.

In the winter of 1955 both George and Jane Palmer had minor strokes and their physicians advised against their continuing to run the camp.

In 1956, Arthur W. Palmer, Jr. and his spouse Mary Jane Palmer, Jane Palmer Barr and her spouse George Barr, and Frances Palmer

Camp Allagash – The Crow's Nest

Fleck and her spouse Richard Fleck; signed a deed releasing any rights they held in the ownership of Camp Allagash to their mother Mary Jane Palmer.

Mary Jane Palmer and Brattan sold the 50-acre property to Peter H.B. and Adaline Frelinghuysen who did not come to Maine but left the business of operating the boys' camp to their grandson Richard Carleton III and his business partner George Williams who ran the camp from 1956 to 1967.

Nathaniel Fleck, whose family had a long history of part ownership of Camp Allagash, was a Camp Allagash counselor from 1962 – 1964 and noted that although some of the boys came from the Philadelphia area, most came from New York City. Carleton was a wealthy individual and paid the camp tuition for many of the New York campers.

Peter H.B. Frelinghuysen died in 1959, and Adaline Frelinghuysen in 1963. Peter and Adaline's grandson Richard Carlton III had received an option from them to purchase the 50 acres of Camp Allagash property at Bolton Cove in 1960. He exercised that option later in 1960, reselling the 50 acres of Camp Allagash back to his grandmother Adaline Frelinghuysen. She died in 1963, and in her will bequeathed the Camp Allagash property to her grandson.

At that point, the Camp Allagash facility had 30 camping sites supplied with water, and ten bunkhouses which could accommodate from 2 to 6 people each and were supplied with beds, cots, and linens. Bunkhouse guests had the use of a large, restaurant-sized kitchen. Additionally, there were six housekeeping cabins with full toilet facilities plus hot and cold running water.

Carlton III had the Camp Allagash property surveyed in 1982, and Mark and Sandra Mathena bought a 27-acre portion of the original Camp Allagash property from him later in 1982. The Mathenas re-opened Allagash as a sporting camp and invited the public to enjoy the former camp sites, buildings, and facilities.

Camp Allagash – The Crow's Nest

In 1985, the Methenas applied for and received a Small Business Administration loan to improve and subdivide the parcel and began the process of developing a residential subdivision. As part of that development, easements were acquired in 2014 for the new five-mile-long Allagash Road to connect with the Burnt Jacket Road which led to the main road between Greenville and Lily Bay. The new road replaced the winding camp access roads to the subdivided lands, and contractor R.C. Whitney and Daughters, Inc. did the work for the project. The Camp Allagash Maintenance Corporation was created to hold the roadway easement rights.[17]

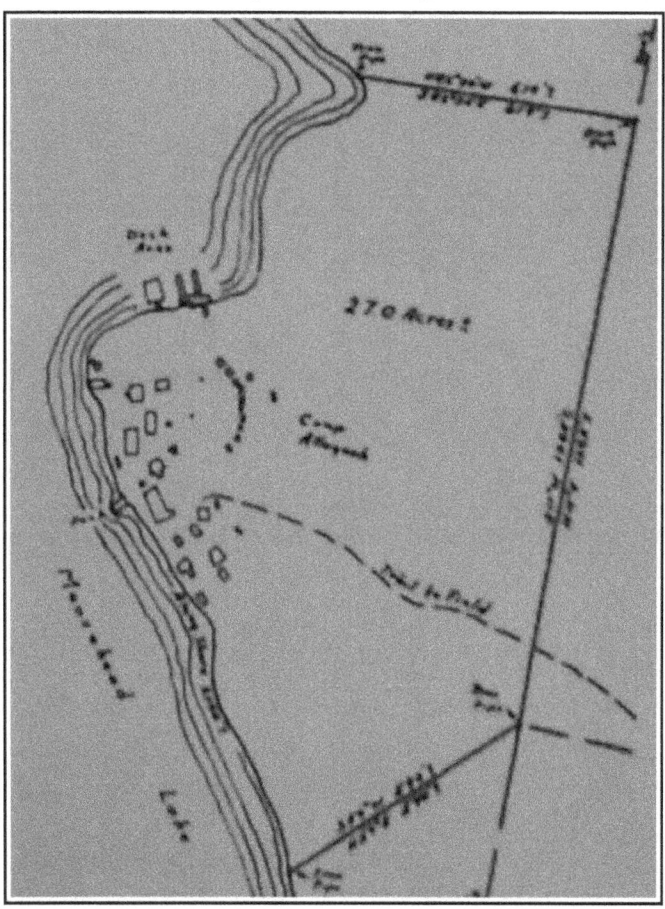

Camp Allagash's 27-acre parcel on Bolton Cove (detail). 1982 Forrest G. Whitman survey, Piscataquis County Registry of Deeds Plan Book G, Page 1.

Beaver Cove Camps

Located on Moosehead's eastern shore, the Beaver Cove Camps property was 2.66 acres in size and was comprised of six log cabins and a 2,400 sq. ft owner's residence.

The camps were on land leased from the J.M. Huber Lumber Corporation until 1966 when Huber created the large "Beaver Cove Cottage Lots" residential subdivision in the Town of Beaver Cove. Vernon and Barbara Davis purchased several lots from Huber in 1966, and gradually sold them to various owners. The Beaver Cove Camps lot was purchased from the Davises by Maurice Pelletier in 1983 and Pelletier sold the property to Alethea Snyder in 1993.

Beaver Cove Camps. google.com/maps/place/Moosehead/Lake

Beaver Cove Camps

These notes on the history of the Town of Beaver Cove are from the Town's website:

> *Founded on March 17, 1975, the Town of Beaver Cove is among Maine's smallest and most beautiful communities. It is located six miles North of Greenville on the eastern side of Moosehead Lake. It spans an area from Moosehead Lake to the Pleasant River and from Beaver Creek to Mud Cove. Some camps along the shores of what is now Black Point Road have been around since the 1920s. Long before there were roads to access the area, hardy residents would tow their small camps across Moosehead Lake from Burnt Jacket Mountain and Bolton Cove in the wintertime onto the Beaver Cove shoreline. Before the town organized, the Huber Lumber Corporation was a major part of the township's existence.*
>
> *Beaver Cove was a designer community of the Huber Lumber Corporation, and actually won an award for the best new community design of the Year! Some original lots along what is now Black Point Road were originally mapped in the late 1950s. Huber designed the community to have a little bit of everything and plotted out the original lots after soil testing. Condos were set up near where the marina is located today, smaller lots were created in the Village Circle area, and larger lots were plotted out on North Ridge and Black Point Roads. The community was set up to provide something to fit every taste. Large lots were plotted out to compensate for having less desirable non-waterfront land. Huber set up two associations for the purposes of controlling and maintaining public lands and beaches. These organizations are called the Beaver Cove Association and the North Ridge Association. Huber also owned what is now the Beaver Cove Marina and associated buildings. The main marina (red) office was originally designed by Huber to be a community house. Difficult economic times during the 1970s resulted in Huber still having half their lots unsold. Much of this unsold land was given to the associations as common land/greenbelt, giving added benefits for the residents.*

The two oldest cabins at the Beaver Cove Camps were built in 1904 and 1905, using vertical log construction instead of the horizontal log construction more commonly seen. At one time there was a central lodge, but that is now privately owned. The six cabins had one or two bedrooms, electricity, indoor plumbing including showers, propane heaters and stoves, an outdoor fireplace, and linens.

Although the cabins had electricity, neither radios nor televisions were allowed in order to create a more unique camp experience and a relaxed atmosphere. Internet service was available, though, because of the requests of some guests for email service, and the importance of the website and reservation systems to the camp itself.

Beaver Cove Camps Office. Facebook.com/MooseheadMemories/photos

Marilyn and Dan Goodwin purchased the camps (648 Black Point Road, Beaver Cove) in 2000 from Snyder. In the Goodwin's era, the six housekeeping cabins offered all the necessities for a comfortable getaway any time of the year. A dock and boat launch facilities were available for their guests, and the cabins were close to the ITS snowmobile trails. Guests enjoyed salmon and brook trout from the lake, and scouted for nearby bear, moose, and deer.

The Goodwins retired in 2016, however, and the camps are now permanently closed.

A Beaver Cove cabin. Beaver Cove Campgrounds website.

The Birches

The Birches camps were launched in 1930 by logging contractor Ozwald "Oz" Fahey to serve French Canadian loggers working in the area and sportsmen seeking lodging for hunting and fishing. In the years of the Great Depression, the logging industry was affected as were many others, yet Fahey still had crews who needed jobs and were willing to work. In 1932, Fahey leased land for The Birches from the Great Northern Paper Co. He made his Moosehead Lake house, just north of the Moose River, into the main lodge, and between 1932 and 1945 built 18 log cabins surrounding it, at the rate of about one per year to create a sporting camp business.

The BIRCHES
On MOOSEHEAD LAKE
Reached by Rockwood-Jackman Highway, R. 195
The most modern log camps in Maine. All the comforts of home in the Big Woods on the shores of Moosehead. Finest trout and salmon fishing on Moosehead Lake.
Joyous vacations for the whole family. Open May 1st to Oct. 1st.
Rates: Lodge $5.00 per day, $30.00 per week. Camps $6.00 per day, $35.00 per week. Special rates to families and parties.
O. R. FAHEY, Prop.   ROCKWOOD, MAINE

Maine Invites You ad, 1933. Maine Publicity Bureau.

Fahey operated the business until 1955, when, due to health issues, he sold it to Harry and Edythe Towle of Cedar Grove, New Hampshire. They ran the camps for the next six years.

The Birches

The BIRCHES
On Moosehead Lake
Rockwood, Maine

A Modern, Luxurious Vacation Lodge for the Discriminating

HERE in one of Maine's few primitive deep woods settings is a group of modern, charmingly rustic cabins and lodge, all directly on the shore of Moosehead Lake. The cabins have the most amazingly comfortable casual furnishings. All have a living room, one or more baths and bedrooms and each has its own private dock and float for sunbathing, swimming, or for canoes and boats. Maid service is provided.

The huge peeled log dining hall makes every meal a relaxed unhurried occasion of complete satisfaction.

Two excellent chefs serve up an inspired array of carefully prepared viands embracing the finest food to be had.

Around the conversation-provoking double fireplace in the lodge our select congenial guests gather for relaxation. They enjoy informal parties, games, and home movies. Also a cozy cocktail lounge on the premises.

All water sports are available and the large T-dock is the center for swimming parties and sports events.

Of course fishing is the main attraction and THE BIRCHES is right in the center of the best fishing grounds on Moosehead. Trout, salmon, and togue are brought in every day throughout the season.

Guides, boats, motors, canoes, and cabin cruisers are available to our guests.

Here is that "out of this world" spot you have been seeking ... on a beautiful crystal-clear lake surrounded by mountains. It is within easy reach by auto or plane. Plane to Bangor. By auto follow R. 15 from Bangor or R. 150 from Skowhegan to Guilford, then take R. 15 to The Birches.

Detailed information and colored brochure on request

Reservations should be made well in advance.

OPEN MAY 15TH TO SEPT. 30TH

R. M. COCHRANE
Manager
Rockwood, Maine
Telephone 534-2151

Maine Invites You ad, 1963. Maine Publicity Bureau.

The Birches

Before opening for the 1962 season, the Towles sold The Birches to Telford Allen, the president of a cosmetics company. GNP Co. and Allen renewed the land lease at $125 annually and extended it until 1977. Allen added a swimming pool, a marina, and a new lounge, but then went broke in 1964. The camps were closed from 1965-1969

John Willard, Sr., and his sons John and Bill bought the complex in 1969, and the GNP Co. land lease was renewed and extended. Willard, Sr. had retired after many years in the dry cleaning and construction business, and scrambled to successfully recondition the buildings for reopening in 1970. Because cooking was one of his hobbies, John, Sr. became the chef at the lodge.

John Willard, Jr. owns and operates the resort business today, and it has expanded activities for guests to include moose cruises twice a day, challenge fitness courses, lake, and whitewater kayaking, sailing lessons, interpretive hiking, cross country ski trails, and snowmobiling.

Willard's Wilderness Expeditions business provides canoe trips and whitewater rafting on the Kennebec and Penobscot Rivers. The Birches' 11,000 acres of private wilderness reportedly makes it the largest activity-based resort in the United States. Willard says that the pattern of each year is ice fishing and snowmobiling from January through March. April is spring cleaning, May through September is open water fishing, rafting, swimming, and other water sports. September and October bring fall foliage, and October and November are hunting season.

The Birches

The Birches shorefront cabins in winter. birches.com.

Dining room at The Birches lodge. birches.com.

The 15 cabins all have names from popular songs of the mid-20th century, such as "In the Mood," "Days of Wine and Roses," and "September in the Rain." The resort also offers "cabin tents" with four beds each for a more rustic experience, but not as rustic as sleeping on the ground.

Birches lodge.birches.com.

The Capen's

Starting in the mid-1830s, lumber became a major Maine industry. During that period, Bangor became known as the Lumber Capital of the World with more than 300 sawmills, and many vessels from both Europe and the U.S. docked daily to be filled with lumber as cargo. Entrepreneurs saw the Maine north woods as a golden opportunity to get in on the ground floor of the burgeoning lumber industry.

General Aaron Capen, of the Capen family that had lived and farmed for several generations in Dorchester, Massachusetts, had become a Brigadier General in 1828. He and his son, Aaron Jr., trekked up from Boston in 1833 to check out timberland investment opportunities in the Moosehead Lake Region. After cruising around the lake, they found that Deer Island (2,500 acres) and neighboring Sugar Island (4,208 acres) with excellent supplies of timber were available. Journals at the Osher Map Library, Smith Center for Cartographic Education, written by Aaron Capen, Jr., report that the Capen's had purchased Sugar Island from E. Crehore, who had bought Sugar Island from the Commonwealth of Massachusetts before 1820. Other accounts say the Capen's purchased the two islands from the state of Maine in 1934.

The General lost heavily in the land deal that involved buying Sugar Island from Crehore and sold the island to cover the loss. His excessive engagement in the land speculation boom that was rampant at the time plunged him so deeply in debt that he was obliged to give up his military career and sell the Dorcester farm.

The Capen's Deer Island timberland investment soon led to their establishment of the Deer Island House. After harvesting the virgin white pine on the island, General Capen gave the real estate to his son Aaron, who, with his wife Caroline Foss of Bridgton, Maine, moved to the island. They cleared and developed a 50-acre farm near the center of the island where soils were less rocky.[18]

The Capen's

The Capen's first hotel had 30 rooms but was destroyed by a fire in 1853. It was quickly rebuilt, and about six individual cabins were added to the site.

HUNTING AND FISHING.

The Deer Island House, Situated on Deer Island, in Moosehead Lake, is ten miles from Greenville, terminus of the Moosehead Lake Division, B. & A. R. R.

There are many deer on the Island, and as fine ones are killed here as in any part of the State. As a fishing resort, it is well known. No better fishing in any part of the Lake than here. The steamer "Tethys" is a new boat for the accommodation of guests of the house, and can be engaged to meet parties at Greenville, if desired. For information concerning rooms, etc., address

ED. A. CAPEN, (P. O.) Capen's, Moosehead Lake, Me.

In the Maine Woods ad, 1901.

In 1888, the General's son Charles Capen purchased the steamer *Tethys (I)* and brought her to Moosehead Lake, where she was used to transport clients who arrived at Greenville Junction on the Bangor and Aroostook Railroad the ten miles from Greenville to Deer Island and return them at the end of their stays. She was 38' long, had a 10' beam, and was also used for fishing parties and otherwise transporting guests for excursions. *Tethys (I)* was damaged on Moosehead Lake when she broke away from her mooring but was repaired and sold to The Great Northern Paper Company and served as a logging towboat. *Tethys (II)* was built in Brewer by Si Leach in 1895 for Charles and was brought to Moosehead Lake on the Bangor and Aroostook Railroad. This 52' boat carried passengers on Moosehead Lake for about 20 years, and in 1916 Capen sold her to the Great Northern Paper Company. (Tethys was the wife of Oceanus, and the Greek goddess who became the mother of all the rivers of the earth.)

Aaron, Jr. died in 1896 and his wife Caroline passed in 1905, and the camp was leased for five years to ex-railroad conductor Frank Gardner.

THE DEER ISLAND HOUSE
AND
FRANK GARDNER'S CAMPS,

Situated on Deer Island, in Moosehead Lake,

Ten miles from Greenville, terminus of the Moosehead Lake Division B. & A. R. R. **Direct steamer connections daily.**

There are many deer on the Island, and as fine ones are killed here as in any part of the State.

As a fishing resort, it is well known. No better fishing in any part of the Lake than here. The steamer "Tethys" is a new boat for the accommodation of guests of the house. For full terms, etc., address

FRANK L. GARDNER,
(P. O.) CAPEN'S, MOOSEHEAD LAKE, ME.

In the Maine Woods ad, 1905.

In 1906, during the final two years of Gardner's lease, the Somerset Railroad extension to the Kineo Station in Rockwood was completed, which had the impact of cutting out the Capen's Hotel's profitable winter business of feeding the crews that carried supplies and equipment from Greenville north on lake ice. For many years, the workers had always stopped at the Capen's for their noontime meal on their way across the lake ice from Greenville to Northeast Carry or Northwest Carry. Because the new Kineo station at Rockwood brought Maine Central Railroad trains 20 miles closer to the two carries than the supply route from the Bangor & Aroostook Railroad terminus in Greenville, the crews preferred to travel north from Rockwood instead of Greenville. Avoiding the 20 miles of blustery and sweeping cold winds they experienced while traversing the iced-over lake from Greenville to Rockwood certainly made sense to them.

In the Maine Woods ad, 1916.

In 1907, Henry Capen, Aaron's eldest son, bought the Deer Island House hotel which had been established by his father, along with the farm from his two brothers Edwin and Charles. When Henry purchased the camp property, he and each of his two brothers kept a lot on which to build individual camps. Henry remodeled the hotel and served as owner and host until his death in 1909.

Henry changed the name from Deer Island House to Capen's because of ongoing mail service confusion with Deer Isle on the Maine coast in Hancock County. After Henry's death in 1909, the hotel was leased to Garnet Gartley for the next ten years until Charles returned from WWI in 1919.

The Capen's

A 1923 ad, showing G.W. Gourley as proprietor, promised the finest trout and salmon fishing on Moosehead Lake. It is true that the waters directly in front of the Capen's on the east shore of Deer Island had long been considered one of the best spots on the lake for fishing. The "narrows" or "thoroughfare" between Deer and Sugar Island almost always offer a lee shore, making fishing possible every day no matter the wind direction. Rates began at $4.00 per day.

The ad also noted that camp bathrooms featured hot and cold running water, open fireplaces, and electric lights. Other amenities were proclaimed to be the best of home cooking with fresh eggs, butter, cream, and vegetables from the Capen's own farm, long-distance telephone service, and daily mail delivery.

The year-round Deer Island Post Office opened at Capen's in 1889 and closed about 1938; thereafter mail went through Wilson's sporting camps at Moosehead Lake's east outlet. The Capen's summer post office operated until July 31, 1943.

In 1938, the 72.77-acre Capen property was sold to Carrie (Capen) and Homer Teal, who sold it in 1943 or 1944 to Carrie's brother Norman L. Capen and his wife Alice; Norman was the fourth generation of descendants of General Capen to own the Deer Island property. Norman, Alice, and Aaron operated The Capen's as an active sporting camp with a dining room and staff of guides, and as a vacation and fishing resort through the 1940s and 1950s. Canoes were available for rent, and other types of watercraft could be rented at the nearby Beaver Cove Marina on the mainland.[19]

The rebuilt hotel, however, was consumed by fire on November 17, 1953. The entire 72.77-acre Capen property was then sold by Aaron in 1953 to Dr. Dale Bouton and Marguerite Bouton of New York. In 1975, the Boutons deeded the property to Dale Bouton, Jr. and Patricia Bouton who remain the current owners.

The Capen's

Dr. Boutin bought Henry Capen's "Grayledge" cottage in 1969, sold it to Joseph Adams in 1982 and his son Garrett Adams is now the owner.

Charles' camp on Gin Point was purchased by Craig and Kerry Hadley in 1985, and they are the current owners. (During the Prohibition era, alcoholic beverages were brought illegally from Canada to Maine, and Gin Point was apparently a transfer location.)

Camp Aaron was sold by Aaron Capen to Louisa Worster in 1973, and the Worster family are still the owners.

Except for the former land and lots once owned by the Capen's, the Hilton Timber Trust owns most of Deer Island.

Camps Caribou - Whileaway - Ogontz

The Ogontz shoreline, about six miles south of Seboomook, was first surveyed by Louis Oakes for timberland owners Hollingsworth & Whitney who delineated lots #1 to #10 in 1895. In 1896, surveyor Turner Buswell plotted an additional 17 lots that were assigned only odd numbers, beginning with lot #11 and extending to lot #43.

Camp Caribou and Camp Whileaway were active sporting camps located on the Ogontz shore, with the private cottages Camp Chenango, Camp Ogontz, and Camp Minong occupying most of the balance of the Ogontz shoreline. Although these five camps were on the mainland, they were reachable only by boat because there was no road access. Several additional small camps were constructed along the shoreline in the 1970s.

Camp Caribou. The first description of development at the site of Camp Caribou is in Charles A.J. Farrar's 1884 book *Moosehead Lake, North Woods Wilderness*. In it, Farrar mentions on page 119 the "W Farm" located just south of where Williams Stream enters the lake.

Frederic S. and Anne T. Snyder purchased lot #21 and the southern half of lot #23 of the Turner Buswell survey, approximately 9 acres in all, from Martha M. Snyder in 1903. Camp Caribou was founded by Frederic and Anne Snyder about 1911.

Rather than being a camp which provided outdoor experience to many clients, the text of the 1911 ad shown on the next page seems to indicate it was primarily a cottage for summer rental.

Moosehead Lake, Maine
CAMP CARIBOU

Summer cottage on lake shore, facing mountains; large, fully furnished; seven chambers, bathroom; hot and cold water, spring water; long distance telephone; bathing; through Pullmans to lake; trout, salmon, and togue; daily mail; rental, five hundred dollars, includes canoes, sailboat, ice, fuel, telephone, and complete equipment. References, photographs, and particulars. F. S. SNYDER, 55 Blackstone St., Boston, Mass.

New Outlook, A Weekly Newspaper, vol. 98, May-August 1911. The Outlet Co., NY.

Camp Caribou in 1939, with a 110' crib and stone pier, the Frazier cabin at left, main lodge/winter quarters and original farmhouse at the center, and guides camp at the far right. Richard Kessler collection.

In 1921, Frederic S, and Anne T. Snyder sold Camp Caribou (lots #21 and the southern ½ of lot #23) to J. Asa and Carolyn Larrabee, who took the existing "W Farm" farmhouse on the lakefront and transformed it into a small resort. Asa Larrabee had been working as a handyman for the owner of nearby private cottage Camp Minong when he purchased Camp Caribou. Larrabee advertised Camp Caribou as:

"Small, quiet, ideally situated on Moosehead Lake.
Daily steamer service to and from the Camp's private wharf.
Fresh vegetables from Camp's gardens.
Plenty of fresh milk and cream.
Modern conveniences designed to be in keeping with big woods."

Asa Larrabee's Business card. Richard Kessler collection.

Charles and Harriet Umsted purchased Camp Caribou from the Larrabees in 1950 and operated it as a sporting camp with capacity for 10-20 guests at a time. They also built the "studio" cabin near the shore to provide "superlative" accommodations for two people and installed a water tower to provide running water to the lodge and cabins. A generator powered the water pump and provided hot water for sports and guests.

Camps Caribou – Whileaway – Ogontz

Camp Caribou's Frazier cabin ca. 1930. Richard Kessler Collection.

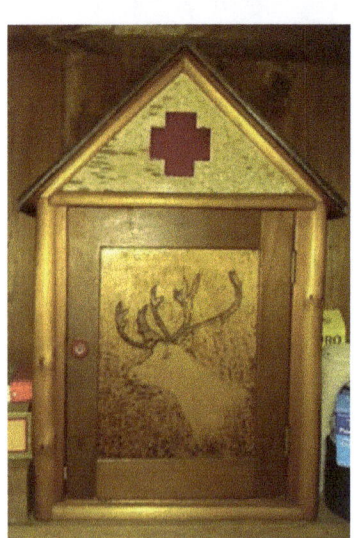
Camp Caribou's first aid cabinet of birch bark and tree limb materials, with a hand carved in a low-relief (or bas-relief) design. Photo by the author.

Low-relief image on a wood panel of the Camp Caribou main lodge living room. Photo by the author.

Camps Caribou – Whileaway – Ogontz

Camp Caribou

is situated on the westerly shore near the remote northerly end of Moosehead Lake, fifteen miles above Rockwood, and offers the fisherman, vacationist and hunter an ideal setting for pursuing the sport of their choice.

For trout, togue and land-locked salmon, Moosehead Lake, of course, is unexcelled. This camp is the nearest to the famous old salmon fishing grounds off Norcross Point and around Duck Cove. From ice-out until late June and again during the month of September, Caribou is run for the convenience of fishermen — as nearly perfect as the host — an ardent fisherman himself, can make it.

A fleet of new, fifteen-foot Midland boats, designed for comfort and safety in heavy weather and completely equipped, are available, as well as Johnson motors for those who do not choose to bring along their own. Canoes, fishing licenses, tackle, bait, gasoline and guides are available at the camp.

FOR LARGE PARTIES OR families, the **Frazier Cabin** is ideal. It has all the seclusion of a private home with none of the cares of housekeeping, as meals are served in the Main Camp. As seen above, both bedrooms have windows facing the lake as well as the woods. A vestibule separates the completely equipped bathroom from the other three rooms. The broad piazza extends the length of the building, forty feet.

Bedrooms in the Main Camp and Winter Building are comfortably furnished — each has at least two windows, facing different directions. Every sleeping room at Camp Caribou is a corner room.

Camp Caribou brochure (detail), Collection of The Moosehead Historical Society #2003.62.0044.

In 1954, the camp was bought from the Umsteds by Herbert and Clare McWilliams. In an (undated) interview by *Bangor Daily News* outdoors columnist Bud Leavitt, Herbert McWilliams described his extensive plans for the camp. They were to … "build a 450-ft. docking area and an operating seaplane base. He is double-fibre-glassing five Midland 15-foot motorboats and will operate a 26-ft.

Camps Caribou – Whileaway – Ogontz

Jonesport cabin launch from Greenville-to-Seboomook-to-Ogontz. ... He'll have his own float plane tied to his dock for quick transportation and a flight to northernmost Maine for back-country angling and gunning. The McWilliams plan to operate twelve months per year. Next winter they will offer ice fishing and winter sports parties."

The McWilliams welcomed guests at the camp until 1962, when they sold the land and buildings to Burton N. Packard, Jr. Packard was a member of the family which owned the famed Packard's Camps on Sebec Lake in Willimantic (near Dover Foxcroft), and Ogontz neighbor Richard Kessler recalls that Packard ran Camp Caribou as a sporting camp for several years. Packard sold the Camp Caribou part of lot #21 and the southern ½ of lot #23 (but excepting the "studio" lot) to Henry Leroy and Margaret Finch in 1967. The Umsteds sold the "studio" portion of lot #21 to Henry and Margaret Finch in 1968.

Dentist Bradford "Doc" C. Godfrey and his wife Isabel bought the lot #19 property, adjacent to Camp Caribou's lots, from Melvin Johnson in 1949 and had a cabin and small boathouse constructed there. (Johnson had acquired ownership of lots #15, #17, and #19 as tax-acquired property from the state of Maine in 1943.) After her husband's death, Isabel Godfrey sold lot #19 and the two buildings to U.S. Air Force Col. Daniel Griffin and his wife Sarah Griffin in 1967.

The Griffins sold lot #19 to Henry LeRoy Finch, Sr., and Margaret Finch in 1983, and their daughter Annie Finch was deeded the lot and the two cabins from her mother in 1999.

Annie Finch writes "My parents Roy and Margaret Finch named the property Camp Cumbers because of the unforgettable Abenaki guide Tom Arsenault, who lived in Rockwood from his boyhood and helped to do a lot of work on Camp Caribou in his later years, in the 1960s. Tommy used to plant cucumbers in the garden at

Camps Caribou – Whileaway – Ogontz

Camp Caribou every spring, which my mother and I would slice and marinate in vinegar to serve at lunchtime. I was about ten years old, and Tommy was very kind to me; he used to bring me gifts and whittle whistles and fans and other toys for me out of wood. Because he knew I loved to eat the cucumbers, he would make a point to wink at me each day as he passed me the bowl and ask, 'Cumbers, Anna?' We named the house in honor of that story."

The two Camp Cumbers cabins owned by Annie Finch are at the left. The 1976 Camp Caribou boathouse is at the far right. Photo by the author.

Henry and Margaret added their son Henry LeRoy Finch III "Roy" to their deed for adjoining lots # 21 and #23 (1/2) in 1993, including Packard's studio cabin. The Finch-owned properties then totaled 12 acres in size.

Caribou was not only a sporting camp, but also served its neighbors with a small store and the Ogontz Post Office (U.S. Postal Service records show it existed from 1928-1956), moved there from its original location in nearby Camp Ogontz. The reason for the long-term survival of the Ogontz Post Office was that Melvin Maynard Johnson, Sr., a distinguished Massachusetts attorney and Grand Master of the Grand Lodge of Massachusetts, and later kept the

Camps Caribou – Whileaway – Ogontz

Ogontz post office solvent by sending large numbers of mailings to the Massachusetts Order of Masons and to Masons in a 15-state district, all to be postmarked from Ogontz (see page 93).

Envelope with 1934 Ogontz Post Office cancellation. Collection of The Moosehead Historical Society.

Richard Kessler recalled hearing that the Post Office was moved from Camp Ogontz to nearby Camp Caribou in the early 1930s when Asa Larrabee was the Caribou owner.

The Ogontz Post Office was a seasonal operation from 1928-1956. When the Ogontz Post Office at Camp Caribou closed in 1956, the mail was delivered by contract postman Clarence Johnson (who was not related to the Ogontz owners Melvin Maynard Johnson and family) by boat from Seboomook. Clarence lived at Seboomook year-round and was a contract mail carrier for the Rockwood Post Office. Richard Kessler remembered that Clarence came three times a week to the camp dock where a box was placed to receive mail and hold outgoing mail for pickup. For a small fee, Clarence would also drop off groceries. Clarence always had at least one dog in his boat and said he kept warm in the winter by having all his dogs sleep on the bed with him.

The remaining contents of the Ogontz Post Office room at Camp Caribou were donated in 2021 by Roy Finch to the Moosehead Historical Society.

Camp Caribou main lodge living room. Collection of Roy Finch.

Camp Caribou main lodge living room with owner Roy Finch in 2022. Photo by the author.

Camp Caribou continues to be owned by **Henry LeRoy Finch III** "Roy" of the Finch family

Camp Whileaway. Camp Whileaway was a sporting camp just south of Camp Caribou, located on lots #11 and #13 (total of about 13 acres) of the 1896 Louis Oakes plan.

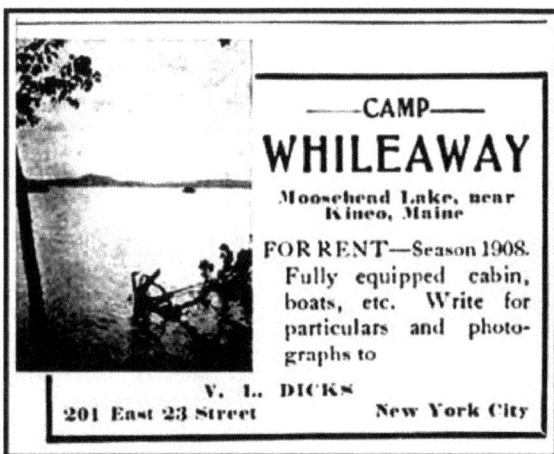

Virginia Dicks purchased lot #11 in the early 1900s and built a cabin there which she named Camp Whileaway. This 1908 ad appeared in the *New York Times* and the *Yale University Weekly* newspaper.

Addie Wickwire and Florence Dawley purchased lot #13 from the Somerset Timberland Co. in 1913.

In 1926, Virginia Dicks' estate left lot #11 to Addie Wickwire who then operated lots #11 and #13 as the Whileaway sporting camp from 1929-1931.

Camp facilities included a main guest lodge with a massive stone fireplace and stone inglenook, guest cabins, a dining room and kitchen, a log recreation building, staff quarters, guides camp, dock, and a vegetable garden and chicken coop. A beach, canoes, and gasoline-powered camp launch were available for guest enjoyment.

In the late 1920s, Whileaway was rented to an association of doctors and nurses from a hospital in New Hampshire who used it as a retreat.

Colgate University professor John Starr and his family rented the Whileaway cottage in the early 1930s, but the years of the Great Depression brought an end to rental uses.

Guest lodge with porch at the left. The building at the right held a dining room, kitchen, and living room with staff quarters above. Richard Kessler collection.

Guest lodge porch closeup. Richard Kessler collection.

The guest lodge contained expansive bedrooms, a large living room with a stone fireplace, and a veranda style porch.

Peeled log cabins were also an option for guests.
Richard Kessler collection.

Camp Whileaway recreation building. Richard Kessler collection.

The separate recreation building held a dance floor, piano, and billiards table.

Wickwire sold the camp and property to Massachusetts couple Ray "Lorne" Greene and Harriet Johnson (no relation to Melvin Maynard Johnson family who owned Camp Ogontz) in 1950. Tragically, Greene and Johnson drowned in Moosehead Lake in December 1950. It was theorized that they were returning to their camp with supplies bought earlier that day in an auto trip to Greenville. In loading their supplies into their small boat at the Seboomook wharf for their return trip to the camp, they broke through the thin ice closer to shore. They had apparently safely traversed the lake ice earlier that day but had moved the boat closer to shore when loading their purchases, and the much thinner ice gave way.

The camp's buildings suffered from deterioration, however, and the main lodge collapsed in the 1950s.

Through Harriet Johnson's bequest, Harriet's father Andrew Johnson became the Whileway owner; his estate sold it to Robert Barr, Sr., and Evelyn Barr in 1969. Robert Barr, Sr. and Robert Barr, Jr. became joint owners in 1982, and Robert Barr, Jr. became sole owner in 1992. The camp's buildings again became vacant, and additional deterioration over the coming years made their demolition necessary.

In 2005, the former Whileaway property (lots #11 and #13) was purchased by Josef Jindra who constructed a large log house on the site and remains its owner.

Camps Caribou – Whileaway – Ogontz

Camp Ogontz. Jay Cooke, Jr.'s deed for the Camp Ogontz property shows that in 1899, he purchased the northern ½ of lot #5 and all of lots #7 and #9 (three adjacent lots) as shown on Oakes' 1896 subdivision plat for the Ogontz shore, from Elias Milliken. Although Camp Ogontz was a private camp and only briefly a commercial sporting camp in the 1950s, it is described here because the current name "Ogontz" for the shoreline derives from Cooke's ownership.

Camp Ogontz was built, about 1899, by American banker Jay Cooke, Jr., the eldest son of Jay Cooke, Sr., the important financial support network financier for the Union during the Civil War. The camp included a 2½ story lodge, a separate kitchen/dining room building, a long narrow guides camp, a boathouse, an icehouse and a spring house, a large vegetable garden, and a shed for the horses that plowed the garden. The pier, built of log cribbing and filled with stone, was extended to 180' by later owner Melvin Maynard Johnson, Sr. to accommodate lake steamboats including the 102' long *Katahdin*, which drew 7½' of water and could carry 500 passengers.

Two important amenities at Camp Ogontz were a seasonal Post Office and a telephone line installed by Cooke, connecting with a GNP Co. line to Seboomook where telephone service was available about 1899. Camp Ogontz neighbor Richard Kessler recalled as a youngster seeing porcelain knobs on trees there and concluded they showed the telephone line's location.

Both Jay Cooke, Sr. and his son Jay Cooke, Jr. were passionate trout fishermen, and were among those who had chartered "The Ogontz Fishing Club" in 1885 and built the Club's "Ogontz Lodge" in Salladasburg, Pennsylvania.

The author toured the Camp Ogontz buildings and site with owners Marta Finch Kozlosky and Charles Kozlosky in August 2022 and noted that the former guides camp was a 24' x 24' log structure 1½ stories in height connected to a narrow ell of sawn lumber some 60' in length. The large size of the guides camp, the arrangement of the kitchen and dining room accommodations, and the nine mounted deer heads in the lodge would lead one to conclude that Camp Ogontz saw considerable sporting activity by guests during its history. The present owners observed that during the period of Johnson ownership (Johnson, Sr. from 1921-57 and his son Melvin Johnson Jr. from 1957-1965), Camp Ogontz was a very active place where the Johnsons entertained business associates and friends.

Camp Ogontz lodge in the early 1900s. hippostcard.com.

Camps Caribou – Whileaway – Ogontz

Camp Ogontz lodge in 2022. Photos by the author.

Camp Ogontz dining room and kitchen building in 2022. Photo by the author.

The idea behind placing the kitchen and dining room in a separate building was to prevent fire danger to the main lodge and control the presence of mice and other rodents.

Jay Cooke, Sr. is best remembered for developing the Union's financial support network during the Civil War by arranging loans for the government and selling bonds, an effort that contributed enormously to the Union victory. As the war progressed, the government issued hundreds of millions of dollars' worth of bonds, and Treasury Secretary Salmon Chase spent much of his time badgering banks and wealthy investors to purchase them. Chase made a partial end run around the bankers with the help of the financier Jay Cooke, who employed 2,500 salesmen to market bonds directly to ordinary Americans.

By war's end, Cooke had sold over a billion dollars in bonds for the federal government. Though Cooke received only a small commission on the sale of the government bonds, his Philadelphia banking house flourished as a result of the trust and acclaim garnered through his ability to finance the Civil War.

Cooke believed that he "could sell the loan on patriotic principles far easier than on the basis of profit & loss," and yet he filled his newspaper ads with promises of stable investments and tax exemption. Principal and interest were patriotic principles, and for better and for worse, Cooke's coupling of individual self-interest and American patriotism forever shaped how Americans have thought about their fiscal obligations in wartime.

From Roger Lowenstein's history "Ways and Means, Lincoln and His Cabinet and the Financing of the Civil War," New York Times Book Review, April 2022.

Camps Caribou – Whileaway – Ogontz

Jay Cooke, Jr.'s involvement with Moosehead Lake is further documented in the "1905 Annual Reports of the Various Departments and Institutions to the Maine State Legislature" by Forest Commissioner Edgar E. King, where he is listed as the 1904 Forest Fire Warden for Big W (which included Camp Ogontz) and Little W Townships. Also, a 1908 stock certificate available for purchase through an online website shows that Cooke, Jr. bought five shares of stock in the Moosehead Lake Yacht Club (located at The Breakwater at the Mt. Kineo Hotel and Resort) at $50 per share.

Although Jay Cooke, Jr. died in 1912, his will bequeathed the camp to his widow Clara A. M. Cooke who continued to use the property. The society pages of the September 1, 1918, edition of the "Philadelphia Inquirer" contained an item saying "Mrs. Jay Cooke, Jr. of 2204 St. James Place is spending some time at Camp Ogontz, Kineo, Maine, and will return the last of September."

The origin of the place name "Ogontz" for that westerly portion of the Moosehead Lake shoreline connects with the Cooke family.

Chief Ogontz. Charles and Marta Kozlosky collection.

Camps Caribou – Whileaway – Ogontz

Chief Ogontz was the leader of the Wyandotte tribe of Ottawa Indians that encamped during the spring months at "Ogontz Place" on Lake Erie (present day Sandusky, Ohio). Chief Ogontz, although not known for his friendliness, was reportedly tolerant of the white settlers and encouraged trade with them.

> *Jay Cooke, Sr., born in Sandusky in 1821, grew up at the site of a lodge once occupied by Ogontz of the Wyandotte tribe. He recalled that Chief Ogontz would visit their home for weeks at a time, delighting the children with tales of "Indian" adventures. Cooke was so impressed with the qualities he found in Ogontz - bravery, loyalty, integrity - that in 1865 he named the lavish and grand mansion he built at Elkins Park, Pennsylvania, "Ogontz."*
> libraries.psu.edu/about/collection/Ogontz-school-1850-1950/cooke-and-chief-ogontz

Jay Cooke, Jr., then, named Camp Ogontz at Moosehead Lake out of the family's deep admiration for the qualities the family found in Chief Ogontz – bravery, loyalty, and integrity.

Jay Cooke's widow Clara A. M. Cooke sold Camp Ogontz (the northern ½ of lot #5, and lot #7 and #9) to Melvin Maynard Johnson, Sr. in 1921. Johnson, Sr.'s biography in the *Who's Who in Maine 1926-27* listed his residences as Beacon Street in Brookline, Massachusetts, and Camp Ogontz, Moosehead Lake, Maine.

The Snyders, owners of Camp Caribou lots #21 and ½ of #23, purchased lots #15 and #17, located between Camp Whileaway and Camp Caribou and then sold the two lots to Robert Mortimer Jones in 1915. Jones devised the Guaranty Trust Company of New York to hold the property for life use by Carrie Hutchins Russell and James Howard Russell. The deed stipulated that after the death of the Russells, the lots would go to the Community Service Society of New York. In the 1930s, the Community Service Society abandoned them because the income from the Jones' estate was insufficient to pay the property taxes. The state of Maine acquired title to those lots, plus lot #19, in 1938 by placing liens against them for the unpaid taxes.

In 1943, Melvin Maynard Johnson, Sr. purchased state tax-acquired lots #15, #17, and #19 (totaling about 26 acres) through the state's Forest Commissioner.

It was Melvin Maynard Johnson who kept the Ogontz Post Office [originally located at Camp Ogontz] a feasible operation by sending prodigious amounts of mailings to the Massachusetts Order of Masons to be postmarked from there.

Postcard of the Ogontz Post Office at Camp Ogontz. Collection of The Moosehead Historical Society #95.4.152 (see note below).

Note: Although the postcard above is labelled as depicting an elegant and comfortable Ogontz Post Office at Camp Ogontz, Edward Rice Johnson, the grandson of Melvin Maynard John, Sr., reported that the Post Office was in a small combination office and woodshed building near the Camp Ogontz kitchen.

Camps Caribou – Whileaway – Ogontz

Edward Rice Johnson noted that the reason his grandfather wanted to have the operation of the Post Office at Camp Ogontz moved to nearby Camp Caribou was because visitors coming to get their mail would seek to chat with him. That became something of an intrusion on his privacy and impacted the time he had available to generate the prodigious amount of correspondence his responsibilities required. He even had a private male secretary working with him at the camp, typing up all his Masonic correspondence right into the 1940s.

Edward Rice Johnson wrote that his grandfather kept Camp Ogontz fixed up in grand style and maintained it for many years. He was able to conduct most of his affairs in that location during late spring, all summer plus early fall, about 3 months in all, and still function as an attorney and stay in touch with the world and his Masonic affairs.

The date of the Ogontz Post Office move to Camp Caribou is uncertain, but past and current owners agree that it probably occurred in the 1930s.

> *One of Massachusetts' best known and most distinguished citizens, Melvin Maynard Johnson, Sr. was educated in the public schools of Waltham, graduating from the high school in 1888. He then entered Tufts College from which he was graduated Ph.B., A.B., in 1892. He graduated from Boston University Law School, LL.B., magna cum laude, in 1895. He was admitted to practice in the Supreme Court of Massachusetts in 1895, the United States Circuit Court in Massachusetts District in 1896, the United States Circuit Court, Connecticut District, in 1901, the United States Supreme Court in 1903, and the Court of Appeals for the District of Columbia in 1931. (Continued on next page.)*

He was associated with his father in the practice of law under the firm name of Johnson and Johnson from 1895 to 1903 and with Johnson and North from 1908 to Dec. 31, 1939, when he retired from the practice of law. He was a lecturer at the Boston University Law School in 1918-1919, Professor, 1920-1935; Dean, 1935-1942, and dean-emeritus of the school. From the New England Craftsman, vol. XXXVIII, No. 8, April 1943.

Richard H. Curtis, writing in the magazine Northern Light, A Window for Freemasonry, *Vol. 31, No. 1, February 2000, named Johnson as "Mason of the Century." He became Grand Master of the Grand Lodge of Massachusetts in 1913, and from 1933-1953 was elected to successive three-year terms as Sovereign Grand Commander of the Supreme Council, Northern Jurisdiction of the Ancient & Accepted Scottish Rite. (The Sovereign Grand Commander performs the role of chief executive officer for the member 15 states in the jurisdiction.)*

Curtis noted that "During the course of summers, he [Johnson] would become a recluse at a small hideaway on Moosehead Lake in Maine. Known as Camp Ogontz, the land could not be reached by auto. Occasionally he would invite select committees to meet with him there to deliberate over important matters. He would have them transported to his camp by boat."

The 102' *Katahdin* at the Camp Caribou pier (or it might be the nearby Camp Ogontz pier) about 1929. Richard Kessler collection.

Camp Ogontz caretaker Elmer Andrews on the Camp Ogontz pier. The dock box shown here is for incoming and outgoing mail, and groceries.
Richard Kessler Collection.

The Johnsons employed Harley Budden and his wife, and later Alma and Elmer Andrews, to maintain the camp buildings and property. The Andrews operated Camp Ogontz as a public fishing camp during the mid-to-late 1950s.

Melvin Maynard Johnson, Jr. inherited Camp Ogontz upon his father's death in 1957. He was able to use the camp for only 2 weeks at a time, flying his family in and out from Augusta via seaplanes to save time. Running a hectic business plus having a family took his focus away from Ogontz. He was also not able to spend money on needed maintenance and the lodge and other buildings gradually began to run down. He kept coming until the fall of 1964 when he and his son Edward were there alone doing research on his latest project. His health failed and he died just months later in January 1965.

His will bequeathed his properties to his wife Virginia Rice Johnson. In 1975, she deeded the three Camp Ogontz lots (northern ½ of lot #5 and all of lots #7 and #9) to son Edward Rice Johnson and his sister Gail Johnson Cronin.

After Johnson Jr.'s death, Virginia Rice Johnson (a well-known tennis player) sold the northern half of lot #15 to Edward and JoAnn Lemos in 1972 and then sold the adjacent southern half of lot #17 to them in 1973. Those properties remain owned by a Lemos family trust.

The southern half of lot #15 was sold to Robert and Karolin Hatch in 1972, who still own the property. The northern half of lot #17 was sold to Roger and Jean Temple in 1973, and ownership remains in a Temple family trust.

Camp Ogontz (northern ½ of lot #5, and all of lots #7 and #9) was purchased from Edward Rice Johnson in 1978 by Marta Finch Kozlosky and Charles Kozlosky who remain the current owners.

Camps Caribou – Whileaway – Ogontz

The place name "Ogontz" was entered into the U.S. Geological Survey's list of geographic names in 1980 but seems to have been in common use after the construction of Camp Ogontz (about 1899).

> *Melvin Maynard Johnson, Jr., born into an affluent Boston, Massachusetts family, was commissioned into the Marine Corps Reserve in 1933 as a Second Lieutenant and completed Harvard Law School in 1934. He was a successful lawyer and taught for a short time at Harvard Law School. However, his life-long interest in firearms soon led him down a different path.*
>
> *Johnson designed a recoil-operated rifle (M1941 Johnson rifle) in 1935, and received four U.S. patents on various design features. He also designed the Johnson Light Machine Gun, derived from the M1941 rifle, which was used in limited numbers during World War II and the M1947 Johnson auto carbine, also derived from the M1941 rifle and M1941 light machine gun.*
>
> *Johnson transferred to the Army Ordinance Corps in 1949 and rose to the rank of Colonel. In 1949, Winchester bought the Johnson Automatics Corporation and Johnson was appointed as weapons consultant* to *the Secretary of Defense in 1951.*
>
> *Johnson's patents were used by Armalite on the AR-10, AR-15, and later M16 rifles. Johnson founded Johnson Arms, Inc.*
>
> *In the 1950s and early 1960s, Johnson served as a consultant to high-ranking munitions leaders in the federal government and numerous civilian industries. He was also well known as a promoter and spokesman for effective small arms, authoring or co-authoring 8 books and some 80 articles on weapons, tactics, and marksmanship.* Wikipedia

Camps Caribou – Whileaway – Ogontz

In addition to Camp Ogontz, there are two other large, privately-owned camps that comprised the Ogontz shoreline:

Camp Chenango ("Shenango"). Owned by the Brautigam family, Camp Chenango is on the north side of Camp Caribou by the mouth of Williams Stream and is composed of two parcels.

Parcel #1: In 1922, the Coburn heirs sold lot #29 (6 11/32 acres) on the 1898 Louis Oakes survey to John and Edna Weber.

Parcel #2: The second parcel was identified as lot #31 on the 1896 Turner Buswell plan of lots. Louise Coburn sold the lot to Samuel Philbrick in 1907, and Philbrick deeded that parcel to John Weber in 1908.

The Webers sold the properties to Herman and Mary Nash Brautigam in 1940. Herman and Mary sold them to co-owners Richard and Anne Brautigam and Richard and Gail Salisbury in 1974. The Salisburys sold their share to Richard and Anne Brautigam in 1985; and in 2011, the Brautigams transferred the property to Camp Chenango LLC. In addition to the main lodge, there are ten small buildings on the site which have been adapted to accommodate stays at the camp by members of the Brautigam family.

Camp Chenango's 42' cabin cruiser *Ouanichi,* built at a Maine coast boatyard in 1912, was acquired about 1942 from Camp Moosehead on Sugar Island (see the Sugar Island chapter). Camp Chenango owners leased the vessel to Camps Caribou and Whileaway to transport guests to and from Greenville.

Ouanichi was pictured in a 1929 ad for **Ann V. D. Slingluff's** Moosehead Camp on Sugar Island. In that year, Slingluff had transferred her camp's operational site from the Nelson Camp at

Sandy Bay to the former Thorofare Camps on Sugar Island. Slingluff's Moosehead Camp operated as a sporting camp from May 15th to June 15th and then served as a residential camp for 50 girls ages 7-14 from July 1st to the end of August. Moosehead Camp closed for good in 1931.

Cabin cruiser *Ouanichi*. Courtesy of Richard Brautigam.

Camp Minong (Aguiden Lodge). Directly south of Camp Ogontz is Camp Minong, a private camp. The 42-acre property, comprised of lots #10,8,6,4,3,2,1 and ½ of lot #5 as shown on the Louis Oakes 1896 survey, was purchased from lumber magnates Milton G. Shaw and Elias Milliken in 1897 by University of Chicago Professor (of Latin) William Gardner Hale and spouse Harriet Swinburne Hale. Ownership of the lots were retained by the Hale family until Hale descendent Jocelyn DePaul gained family agreement to sell the land and buildings in 1959 and conveyed them to Mary Starr Kessler in 1961. Robert Day and Mary Starr Kessler Day deeded the properties to the Kessler family children in 1986; and the property was transferred to a Kessler family entity, Aguiden Lodge LLC, in 2013.

Folsom Farm

The Folsom Farm in Days Academy Grant on the eastern shore of Moosehead Lake became the home of Levi (1838-1917) and Evelyn Packard Folsom and their six children (ages 6 to 17) in 1884. They had cleared the land in 1883 with axes and crosscut saws, and their nearest neighbors were about a half-mile south.

Original farmhouse with peeled log construction (detail).
From *The Folsom Farm*, by Dorothy Folsom Weymouth, 1999.

Folsom Farm with the 1895 "Big House" at the center in 1903.
From *The Folsom Farm*, by Dorothy Folsom Weymouth, 1999.

After springtime planting, Levi was a summertime guide, often for the Mt. Kineo Resort or for the Fox family who had camps at Socatean on the lake's western shore. He developed a wide

Folsom Farm

acquaintance among sportsmen and woodsmen who frequented the Moosehead region, guiding many parties of sportsmen on their trips into the northern Maine wilderness, furnishing his own canoe, tent, and equipment for outdoor living and cooking. For Levi, wintertime meant timber harvesting operations.

In 1909, the State Legislature had authorized construction of a road between the Smith Farm near Kineo to Northeast Carry, but the only portion ever constructed was the 12 miles from Kineo to the Folsom Farm.

Often teams of horses and sleds would cross the ice from Northeast Carry to the Folsom Farm and pick up the land route from there.[20]

Woody Bartley, in *The Moosehead Gazette* edition of July 1951, recalled his daily mail service route carrying supplies and passengers. Starting from Greenville Junction, with a noontime dinner 12 miles up the lake at The Capen's on Deer Island, he and passengers arrived at either the Folsom Farm or sometimes Northeast Carry at suppertime. In the winter, people stopped at the Folsom Farm on their way to or from Northeast Carry by stage (horse drawn sleds) for food and Sarah Folsom Huff's warm biscuits.[21]

Winter travelers in a U.S. Mail stage going to or from Northeast Carry. From *The Folsom Farm*, by Dorothy Folsom Weymouth, 1999.

The Folsom's farmhouse buildings were sometimes called the "Halfway House" because they were about midway between Rockwood and Northeast Carry and served as a convenient stopping-off point for sports and lumbermen who needed shelter and attention to logging injuries, or wintry weather for which they were unprepared. The largest number of "stragglers" on the lake during winter conditions who found shelter there was 54.[22]

Little House (detail). Collection of The Moosehead Historical Society #2016.31.0038.

This 1911 photo shows the "Little House" at Folsom Farm. It was used by several different Folsom families over the years, and school was held in the front room. In the 1930s, Mary Folsom rented it to sports and vacationers to supplement family income.

The historic Folsom Farm was destroyed by fire on March 13, 1999. Bill Folsom and his wife had been using it for ice fishing earlier that day, and a caller who noticed the flames from across the lake at the "Toe of the Boot" that evening reported the fire. Rockwood Fire Chief Joe Munster responded across the ice by truck with a portable pump and hoses, and about eight volunteer fire fighters from Rockwood responded by snowmobile, but there was nothing left to save.

Folsom Farm

Phyllis Kirkwood Folsom, 86, of Greenville died May 25, 2005, in Lewiston. She was born August 8, 1918, in Rockwood, the daughter of Hugh Forrester and Stella (Johnson) Kirkwood. She married Howard L. Folsom of the Folsom Farm in 1939 and lived on Moosehead Lake most of her life. She was survived by two daughters, Dorothy Weymouth and husband, Peter, of Auburn and Blanchard, and M. Nancy Weed of Scarborough, and two sons, William Robert Folsom and wife, Karen, of Rockwood, and Thomas Roy Folsom and his wife, Dianne, of Presque Isle.[23]

The Folsom Farm on the eastern shore of Moosehead's north bay is currently for sale. Tom Folsom is the fourth-generation family member to own the property, which consists of three 5-acre surveyed lots. Lot A has a fully furnished, modern, and well-insulated one bedroom camp that, with a loft sleeping space, can sleep up to six. It has propane gas lights and appliances, a Vermont Castings wood stove, and a screened porch which gets the morning and early afternoon sun. The property is served by a modern shed with a composting toilet and has a licensed primitive gray water disposal system. Water is from a productive dug well. The property is surrounded by conservation easements so it will always be quiet and private.

Gilbert & Coombs - West Outlet Camps - Old Mill Campground

The Gilbert & Coombs West Outlet Camps at the west outlet of Moosehead Lake began operating around 1900 on land leased from the Great Northern Paper Co.

In the Maine Woods ad, 1901.

Gilbert & Coombs – West Outlet Camps – Old Mill Campground

These camps were known as West Outlet Camps and were said to be the largest and most up-to-date camps in Maine, offering all the comforts of home. Camp facilities included a large main lodge, 29 guest camps, and numerous smaller cabins, all of log construction.

Gilbert and Coombs Camp, West Outlet, 1905 postcard (detail). Collection of The Moosehead Historical Society #2000.0661.

Hiram Coombs was a respected guide and for 22 years served as captain the Mt. Kineo resort boats. Coombs partnered with his sister Sarah Elizabeth Coombs and her husband Thomas William Gilbert, who had married in 1894. Coombs' sister, Alice, was also part of the team that ran the camps as Gilbert & Coombs from 1900-1922. Gilbert was a proprietor of the camps for 20 years and died in 1935.

Maine Invites You ad, 1939. Maine Publicity Bureau.

The camps were sold to Frank Mackenzie in 1922 and were then known as MacKenzie's West Outlet Camps. A 1949 *Maine Invites You* ad describes the West Outlet Camps as having "All the Conveniences of the City in the Heart of the Big Woods." Twenty-five comfortable log cabins, central dining room, good food, delightful scenery, excellent fishing, guides, motor boating, canoeing, swimming, and all outdoor activities were available for every member of the family. The camps were open from May 1st to October 1st. Taxi service from Pittsfield, Newport, or Bangor was provided by individual arrangement. Float plane services were available for fishing at remote ponds and streams.

MacKenzie acquired title to the seven-acre West Outlet Camps site in 1947, and in 1959 sold the land and camps to Malcolm and Delores Maheu. Later that same year, the Maheus deeded the camps and property to Ellsworth and Arlene Thompson. The Thompsons sold the camps to Burton Packard and Vivian Packard of the well-known Packard's Camps of Sebec Lake in 1967, and the Packards also purchased 30 acres of adjacent property from GNP Co.

The Packards sold the camp buildings and property to Richard and Kathleen Annunziato in 1978, who renamed the site the "Old Mill Campground," serving a clientele who were primarily retirees and wanted to spend their leisure time boating and fishing while camping at the beautiful pristine camping sites on Moosehead Lake.

The campground offered 56 RV and camping sites, a camp store, hot showers, laundry, game room, and picnic tables that were available to the campers. Also, a variety of boat, canoe, and kayak rentals were offered, and a 75-slip marina was constructed for privately-owned boats. Boaters, ATV riders, and snowmobilers found the camp services to be convenient and affordable.

Maine Invites You ad, 1983.
Maine Publicity Bureau.

The Annunziatos sold the 37-acre parcel to West Outlet LLC in 1999. and the campground was closed. The new owner planned to use the site for a single-family group.

Gray Ghost Camps

On the Moose River, one mile above the Rockwood bridge on Route 15, are the Gray Ghost Camps. Silas Milner appears to have been the camp's founder, having purchased the property from Louise Coburn in 1899. Milner sold the camps to Sheldon and Wilma Sawyer in 1951. After a succession of owners, Roger and Jane Lane purchased the camps in 1974 and kept the cabins open year-round to accommodate wintertime snowmobilers, skiers, and ice fishermen. Steven Lane, a registered Maine Guide and private pilot, purchased the camps in 1999, and he and wife Amy Lane are the owners of the camps today.

Fishing on Moosehead Lake and the Moose River is featured, as is area fly fishing in June and September. Exploring the north woods to fish on secluded streams is also recommended to guests.

Gray Ghost Camps are at the lower left in this 1940s photo.

Twelve "housekeeping" cabins comprise the camps, all completely furnished and with modern facilities including propane heat, refrigerator, blankets, pillows, shower, and hot and cold running water. Each has knotty pine paneling, is fully insulated, and located on the waterfront.

Gray Ghost Camps. Photo by the author.

Before the purchase of the property by the Sawyers in 1951, a campground occupied the Moose River site. The Sawyers, though, began building cabins, and named their business Gray Ghost Camps, a name which recognized both their hometown of Gray, Maine, and the famous, classic fishing lure.

Gray Ghost Camps

The **Gray Ghost** streamer fly is an artificial fishing lure of the streamer fly type, designed to imitate live smelt.

www.georgesrivertu.org

Over the years, the camps have offered RV trailer sites with electrical hookups, too, but present owners Steve and Amy Lane are retiring the few remaining sites from future availability.

In 2007, Steve and Amy doubled the capacity of the camps by purchasing six adjacent cabins from Joseph and Hilda King. That

change, plus the addition of remote outpost properties on Sebec Lake, the Piscataquis River, and the East Branch of the Penobscot River, has tripled the camps' capacity.

Gray Ghost has always offered docking facilities, sold gasoline, and rented boats and motors. Roger Lane is semi-retired, and from May to September operates a growing pontoon boat rental business.

Steve and Amy also managed the trail grooming and operations of the local Blue Ridge Riders Snowmobile Club from 2000-2015, and in 2015 Steve became a member of the Blue Ridge Riders ATV Club where he oversees trail maintenance and landowner relations.

Gray Ghost Camps

In 2012, Amy, who is a licensed real estate agent, formed the nonprofit that led to the re-opening of the local ski resort at nearby Big Moose Mountain.

The Lanes' two teenaged sons, the 5th generation of the family which maintains its Rockwood roots, are now involved in the day-to-day operations of the camps.

Pilots of the seaplanes shown here stay at Gray Ghost Camps during the International Seaplane Fly-In held each September that attracts thousands of people to Greenville and the Moosehead Lake region. Pilots compete in contests of skill and enjoy the fall scenery and camaraderie.

All photos are from the Gray Ghost Camps Facebook.com. pages, except where noted.

Camps Greenleaf - Sugar Island - Thorofare - Moosehead - Porcupine - Wilderness Lodge - Eagle Haven

Sugar Island, Moosehead's largest island, is located about eight miles north of Greenville. At 4,208 acres in size, the island is roughly four miles long and two miles wide. The Island is mainly accessed through Lily Bay State Park's boat ramps, and it takes about five minutes to reach the island. From the 1890s until about 1960, a succession of five camps (Greenleaf, Sugar Island, Thorofare, Moosehead, Eagle Haven, and the Wilderness Lodge), plus the private Porcupine and Nighthawk Clubs, have occupied sites on the island.

Brothers Charles D. and William M. Shaw, sons of lumber baron Milton G. Shaw, purchased Sugar Island in 1889 and retained ownership until about 1909. The Shaws deeded the island to timber company Hollingsworth & Whitney (H&W) except for some privately owned lots sold previously. State property assessment records for 1914 show that H&W owned all of Sugar Island except for 37 acres of private property: Elgin Greenleaf's Camp Greenleaf leased lot of eight acres, the Nighthawk Club lot of one-acre, the Porcupine Club camps lot of three acres, the W. M. Shaw lot of ten acres, the H.W. Stafford lot of three acres, the Mary Swigert lot of five acres, the J.H. Perry lot of four acres, and the George Rimbach lot of three acres.

Camp Greenleaf. Camp Greenleaf was established when, about 1901, Elgin A. Greenleaf leased from H&W the eight-acre site at Sugar Island's Birch Point. By 1908, Camp Greenleaf included several large, detached lodges near the main camp, and provided fine table fare, daily mail, telephone, and a private launch for guest transportation.

Camps Greenleaf – Sugar Island – Thorofare – Moosehead – Porcupine – Wilderness Lodge – Eagle Haven

An advertisement proclaimed: "Positively no flies, gnats, or mosquitos here."

In the Maine Woods ad, 1910.

Greenleaf operated the camp for about 10 years, but turned the management over to A.E. "Bert" Van Skoik around 1911. Early advertisements for Camp Greenleaf advised that travel from Boston to Sugar Island took only 14 hours, with the journey from Boston to Greenville by rail, and from Greenville to the camps by steamer. Boston passengers boarded a train at night with Pullman (sleeper) car service and reached the camp at about noontime the following day.

Camps Greenleaf – Sugar Island – Thorofare – Moosehead – Porcupine – Wilderness Lodge – Eagle Haven

By 1906, a train could also be taken from Boston or New York to Kineo Station at Rockwood via the Somerset line which ran from Waterville/Oakland, Maine. Camp Greenleaf provided steamboat transportation which would reach the camp itself during the afternoon.

Camp Greenleaf main lodge. Image Courtesy Moosehead Historical Society 2001.23.000.

Camp Greenleaf postcard. Collection of the author.

Camps Greenleaf – Sugar Island – Thorofare – Moosehead – Porcupine – Wilderness Lodge – Eagle Haven

Van Skoik continued as proprietor of the seven Camp Greenleaf log cabins until 1923, when he was succeeded by William C. Meservey. In 1925, the proprietors were Meservey & Bridge.

Steamer *Priscilla* at Camp Greenleaf dock. Facebook.com /Moosehead Memories/photos

Meservey, assisted by his capable wife Blanche, expanded the number of log cabins to ten after 1926. They could accommodate from two to twelve each and were equipped with "modern conveniences." Meservey operated the camp through 1935.

Ads promised moose, deer, and small game in abundance, and guaranteed a shot at a deer. There were many good trails for hiking, phenomenal fishing, and excellent table fare. Passenger and mail service was provided every day except Sunday.

The Sugar Island Post Office, a "summer" office, operated from March 13, 1906, to January 31, 1942.

Features of the camp included open fires, "bathing," and on-site tennis courts. Motorized boats, row boats, and canoes were available for hire, and hiking and mountain climbing opportunities were nearby. Rates were $4.50 to $5.00 per day, based on the

Camps Greenleaf – Sugar Island – Thorofare – Moosehead – Porcupine – Wilderness Lodge – Eagle Haven

number in camps and the length of the stay. Boarding costs for guides were $2.00 per day.

In the Maine Woods ad, 1926.

"Table" consisted of the best of fresh food, home cooked under the supervision of an expert cook, and nicely served. Milk and cream were from their own tested cows.

Elgin Greenleaf died in 1935, and his estate bequeathed the camps to Harry Greenleaf who managed them for a few years. Harry Greenleaf died in 1947.

Camps Greenleaf – Sugar Island – Thorofare – Moosehead – Porcupine – Wilderness Lodge – Eagle Haven

Sugar Island Camps. From 1949 through 1960, Chandler Robbins, Jr. and Anne Robbins owned and operated the Sugar Island Camps. The camp's assemblage of buildings included a lodge and office, a central dining room where all meals were served, and ten log cabins of varied sizes which could accommodate from two to 12 guests. All cabins had running water, flush and lavatory, were comfortably furnished, heated with open fires, and were kept exceptionally clean.

Maine Invites You ad, 1952. Maine Publicity Bureau.

Camps Greenleaf – Sugar Island – Thorofare – Moosehead – Porcupine – Wilderness Lodge – Eagle Haven

Facebook.com/MooseheadMemories/photos

The Robbins sold the Camp Greenleaf property and buildings to Herbert Cochrane in 1960. Arthur Geetersloh and Michael Vallant purchased the land and buildings from the Cochrane estate in 1987, and in 1990 Geetersloh and Vallant conveyed the property to the Sugar Island Trust. The Trust's three original co-trustees were Arthur Geetersloh, Jr., Michael Warren, and Warren Cochrane, Jr. Trustees Tristan P. Cochrane, and Erik E. Cochrane were added in 2019, and the Trust remains the owner of the property.

Thorofare Camps. The private Nighthawk Club was established about 1891, and its camps were located on the western side of Sugar Island, nine miles north of Greenville. Its location was about a mile north of Camp Greenleaf on a one-acre site leased from William M. Shaw.

William M. Shaw sold the one-acre property the Nighthawk Club had leased to Theron Heald in 1910.

The Nighthawk Club site and buildings had essentially been abandoned after the club dissolved in 1922, and property owner

Camps Greenleaf – Sugar Island – Thorofare – Moosehead – Porcupine – Wilderness Lodge – Eagle Haven

Heald then established the Thorofare Camps there and operated them as proprietor from 1922 to 1926.

In the Maine Woods ad, 1922 -1926.

Heald died in 1930, and his Thorofare Camps were followed by the Moosehead Camps (1929-1931)

Moosehead Camp. In 1929, Ann von Slingluff transferred her Moosehead Camp from the Nelson camp at Sandy Bay to Sugar Island, leasing Heald's Thorofare Camps site. Von Slinghuff's Moosehead Camp served as a sporting camp from May 15th to June 15th, and then as a residential summer camp for up to 50 girls ages 7-14 until the end of August. The camp returned to serving hunting and fishing clientele for October and November. It operated, however, for only the 1929 to 1931 seasons.

In 1932, Heald's widow sold the property, buildings, and wharf to Fred Webster. Webster's widow, Florence, conveyed the property and buildings to Sophie Broadhead in 1944. Donald and Sophie Broadhead first operated the site as the Wilderness Lodge and later incorporated the business as The Wilderness Club, Inc. As of 2020, the property remained in the ownership of The Wilderness Club, Inc. (see the Private Sporting Clubs chapter).

Camps Greenleaf – Sugar Island – Thorofare – Moosehead – Porcupine – Wilderness Lodge – Eagle Haven

Wilderness Lodge. Across the "thoroughfare" from Capen's on easterly side of Deer Island, Donald and Sophie "Barbara" Broadhead owned and operated a sporting camp on the westerly side of Sugar Island. Donald A. Wilson, in his 2006 book *The History of East Outlet, Moosehead Lake, Maine and Wilson's on Moosehead Lake*, describes the Wilderness Lodge or Wilderness Club, Inc. as being able to accommodate only a limited number of patrons at a time, but it was a thriving business from the 1950s to the early 1960s.[24]

In the Maine Woods ad, 1929.

Camps Greenleaf – Sugar Island – Thorofare – Moosehead – Porcupine – Wilderness Lodge – Eagle Haven

In 1930, Clayton Bayard, through the Bayard Outing Club, Inc. of Orono, Maine, purchased the 4-acre "Hazel Point" lot adjacent to the Nighthawk lot from H&W. Donald Broadhead bought the Hazel Point parcel from Bayard in 1945 and sold it to Annie Dwyer that same year. The Broadheads purchased the adjacent "Battery Point" property about 1951 and repurchased the Hazel Point lot in 1961 to add to the "Battery Point" property. They incorporated their business as the Wilderness Club, Inc. in 1963.

Maine Invites You, 1955. Maine Publicity Bureau.

Don was a pilot with his own plane and flew fishing parties to remote lakes and ponds in northern Maine and Canada. There have been several owners since, but as of 2020 the property owners have retained the Wilderness Club, Inc. name.

Porcupine Club Camp. The Porcupine Club camps (see the Private Sporting Clubs chapter) were established on a 2-acre parcel in 1900 (Frank Hall survey) on the easterly side of Sugar Island, to which was added a second, adjacent two-acre parcel in 1906 (Elmer Bowley survey). No details concerning the Club membership have been found.

Camps Greenleaf – Sugar Island – Thorofare – Moosehead – Porcupine – Wilderness Lodge – Eagle Haven

but this 1915 sales ad describes the 4-acre property with four log cabins as being a hunting and fishing camp. The Club may have had only limited success because its site was offered for sale in 1915.

FOR SALE
Hunting and Fishing camp of the Porcupine Club on Sugar Island, Moosehead Lake, Maine. 4 log buildings, with private dock, and about 4 acres of ground, all heavily wooded. 6 double beds, 2 cot beds, 6 guide bunks. All completely furnished with linen, blankets, crockery, glassware and kitchen ware. Also 1 canoe and 1 row boat. Price $5000.00 cash. Possession at once.
Apply to W. I. Babcock, 17 State St., N. Y.

Recreation magazine ad, June 1915.

The property was sold by the club to shipbuilder Captain Samuel Percy of Bath in 1919, and the sale included five log cabins, a pier, and a boathouse. (see the Private Sporting Camps chapter for greater detail.)

From that point onward, the camps were not used to serve hunting and fishing sports or other guests. Percy's daughter, Eleanor Irish, acquired them from the Percy estate in 1940, and she conveyed them to Chester and Anna McCabe in 1944.

The McCabe family members retained ownership of the lots through two generations but listed the Porcupine camps property for sale in 2020. It was purchased in 2021 by Daniel Ross and Peter and Cynthia Arntson, with Ross and the Arntsons each owning ½ interest in the property and buildings.

Camps Greenleaf – Sugar Island – Thorofare – Moosehead – Porcupine – Wilderness Lodge – Eagle Haven

2021 Porcupine Camp boathouse. (Note the faint "Porcupine Camp" sign over the porch.) Real estate website photo.

Eagle Haven Camp

Camp Eagle Haven for the physically handicapped was located on the westerly shore of Sugar Island, and operated by Wanna R. Eagle, wife of Chief Henry Red Eagle [Henry Gabriel Perley] (see the Guides chapter). He met Wanna, a professional diver and swimmer, while working at Coney Island's Dreamland amusement park and she returned to Greenville with him. Eagle Haven camp began operating in 1944 and Wanna purchased the property from Susie Parks in 1947. An Eagle Haven brochure explained that "Mrs. Eagle's own method [of] Specialized Swimming for the Physically Handicapped has been acclaimed by both physicians and members of her classes. Her work has received extensive publicity in the New York press." Her therapies were especially suited for and directed to victims of polio. Other camp courses offered were in fishing, boating, and wildlife. She died in 1969 and her son Henry Perley sold the three-acre property to John and Edna Goodwin in 1972. The

Camps Greenleaf – Sugar Island – Thorofare – Moosehead – Porcupine – Wilderness Lodge – Eagle Haven

property is currently owned by the Orthopedic Associates of Virginia Ltd, Employee Stock Ownership Plan Trust.

Timber Harvesting. Timberland and lumber company owner Milton "M.G." Shaw purchased Sugar Island from the state of Maine in the late 1840s. Deeds for lots sold by Shaw on the island included a stipulation giving him and his heirs or assigns the right to enter onto the island at any time for the purpose of cutting any pine, spruce, or juniper as long as no slash was left behind.

Although it appears that the wood harvesting clause was never effectuated by Shaw himself, hardwood logs on the island were harvested periodically for veneer wood by Shaw's sons Charles D. and William M. They had purchased the island from their father in 1889 for $17,000 and owned it until about 1909 when they sold it to the Winslow-based Hollingsworth and Whitney Paper Company (H&W). (The sale to H&W exempted the 37 acres of private lots described earlier in this chapter.)

With the acquisition of the H&W by the Scott Paper Company in 1954, Sugar Island became the property of Scott Paper. Timber harvesting took place on the island from the mid-1960s through the early 1970s, when softwood pulp and hardwood grade logs were either skidded or trucked directly across the ice to the mainland. After ice-out, some of the pulpwood was towed in booms up the lake to the east outlet through which it was floated down the Kennebec to the Scott Paper's mill in Waterville/Winslow.

Except for the privately owned camp lots on the island which were exempt from the sale, Sugar Island was sold by Scott Paper to the state of Maine in 1985. The island is now managed by the Maine Bureau of Parks and Lands (BPL), which has established six state-authorized tenting sites there.

By 2013, timber on the island had matured again to harvestable dimensions. Typically, the BPL sought competition for timber harvesting on state-owned lands by bidding out the timber harvesting work. However, a contract was negotiated in 2013 with the South

Camps Greenleaf – Sugar Island – Thorofare – Moosehead – Porcupine – Wilderness Lodge – Eagle Haven

African Pulp and Paper Industries Ltd. (SAPPI), which now owns Scott Paper's former Somerset Mill in Skowhegan/Hinckley on the Kennebec River. SAPPI signed a contract to harvest 40,000 cords of Sugar Island hardwood pulp over an eight-year period, with the special condition that to avoid the pollution of lake water with tree bark and soil, the pulpwood would be barged to the mainland and trucked overland to the Somerset Mill. The harvesting plan called for logging to be done only from summer through early fall, and several miles of summer roads were to be constructed on the island and the access road on the mainland rebuilt. A temporary dock system would be installed each spring and removed in the fall. Best Management Practices were critical due to the proximity of the wood harvesting operation to the lake.

E. J. Carrier Logging, based in Jackman, Maine, was selected as the harvester and brought a barge to the site to transport loaded trucks to the mainland.

Camps Greenleaf – Sugar Island – Thorofare – Moosehead – Porcupine – Wilderness Lodge – Eagle Haven

E.J. Carrier Logging's pulp truck, dock system, and barge.

Ross Caron, *Northern Woodlands* magazine, internet posting of May 26th, 2019.

Kokad-Jo Inn - Roach River House - Kokadjo Cabins & Trading Post

Kokadjo is a shorthand form of "Kokodjeweemgroasbem," the Wabanaki word for the Roach River. The name "Roach" River is thought to have been derived from French Canadian priest Father LaRoche who ministered to the native Wabanaki in the region. Some written references to the river, even into the 1930s, spelled its name as the "Roche" River.

The first building at Kokadjo, at the foot of First Roach Pond, was a logging camp built by Enoch "Deacon" Ford, who had moved there in 1841 as a logger from his hometown of Mayfield in Somerset County. Ford had been a deacon in the Mayfield Freewill Baptist Church and served as town selectman and postmaster in 1836.[25]

In 1844, Ira Wadleigh of Old Town bought Township 1 Range 13 (Kokadjo) from the state land agent. Five years later, he sold lots #3 and #9 on what would become known as the Roach River farm to Thomas J. Grant (land that Ford was already farming) although Wadleigh held the mortgage.

The ownership of the farm remained with the Thomas J. Grant family during the decades of the 1850s and 1860s. The family had apparently hired Ford to run the operation, because he moved his wife and children to the farm where they had 100 cleared acres.[26]

During this period of land transactions, Ford also continued to operate what was known as the Deacon Ford "shanty."[27]

Kokad-Jo Inn – Roach River House – Kokadjo Cabins & Trading Post

> *Maine author and historian Bill Geller explains that a "shanty" was like a tavern in purpose, but much more crude. When teamsters toted supplies to the logging camps, the oxen, and later horses, typically pulled a loaded sled about 10 miles per day. So these shanties were generally at 10-mile intervals on the main tote roads. Many, but not all, were year-round farms that raised crops and animals to feed the horses and the teamsters spending the night. The shanty did not always have a hovel [for the oxen or horses]. A shanty could have 10-40 teamsters a night - some going in and others out. They provided meals and lodging for whatever number showed up each day. The men slept hip-to-hip on the floor or in a gang bunk built-in under the eaves.*

Following Ford's death in 1868, the Reuel and Ann Keene family of Augusta took over the farm's operations.

In 1875 James Edwin Grant sold the property back to Ira Wadleigh, who then sold to his granddaughter Sarah Hoskins. She sold a quarter share to her sister Evelyn B. Hoskins, so they owned it jointly. They sold to Samuel H. Blake of Bangor in 1879 and he immediately sold to Elbridge Hunting of Corinth. Hunting continued his ownership through the 1880s, and after Hunting's death in 1892, his family sold their share to Hunting's partner John Morrison (or Morison) who continued ownership of the farm through the rest of the decade. Morrison, a well-known lumberman of Corinth, whose father and brother had a large lumbering operation in the area, had married Enoch Ford's sister, Eliza Jane.[28]

In 1889, Morrison enlarged the Roach River House to 30 rooms with a capacity of 74 guests and built two "cottages," which were two stories high with verandas and were connected to the main house with covered platforms. Hunting became the first postmaster of Roach River in 1890 (or 1895, as records differ). Guests arrived at Lily Bay, often aboard the steamers *Henry M.* or *Louisa*, and Morrison ran a stage line to transport them about seven miles to the Roach River House. His son, Abner Ford Morrison, ran the hotel at least until 1899.

Kokad-Jo Inn – Roach River House – Kokadjo Cabins & Trading Post

In 1900, Morrison deeded the farm to his son, Abner, who operated it for a year.

Roach River House, ROACH RIVER, MAINE.

THIS excellent Hotel is located at the foot of Roach Pond, six miles from Lily Bay (reached from there by a fine buckboard line through a picturesque region), and, with the two cottages under the same management, furnishes excellent accommodations for tourists, sportsmen and their families.

The houses are well furnished and have all home comforts. The table is supplied with the best the market affords, served in a manner that pleases every one. The location at the foot of Roach Pond, which it overlooks, is very desirable. This pond is six miles long, surrounded by others, with lakes and streams in every direction which are full of gamy trout; and it is a fact that within a few rods of the veranda of the house is one of the finest trout pools in the State. In the open season there is game in great variety – moose, caribou, deer, bear, partridge, ducks and other small game, which cannot fail to satisfy all lovers of rod and gun; and to those who are seeking health and quiet rest the grand mountain scenery, cool spring water and pure air must prove indeed a blessing. The management furnishes guides, boats, canoes and complete camping outfits.

The route to reach here is via the **Bangor & Aroostook Railroad to Greenville Junction**, twice daily from **Boston or Maine Central R. R. Points**, or via the **Canadian Pacific Railway** from the East or West. Connections are made here with steamers which leave daily (Sundays excepted) on arrival of morning train from Bangor, connecting at Lily Bay with Frank P. Morrison's Line of Buckboards for Roach River. RETURNING (Sundays excepted,) leave Lily Bay for Greenville Junction, connecting with afternoon train for Bangor and the West. **Daily Mail Service.**

A. F. MORRISON, Proprietor, ROACH RIVER, ME.

Abner Ford Morrison's ad in *Carleton's Pathfinder and Gazetteer of the Hunting & Fishing Resorts in the State of Maine, 1899.*

In 1901, Abner Ford Morrison sold the 600-acre farm, the Roach River House hotel, and the two cottages to Elizabeth J. Sawyer of Bangor, and she and her husband Charles H. Sawyer successfully ran the Roach River House for seven years. Charles Sawyer was also

Kokad-Jo Inn – Roach River House – Kokadjo Cabins & Trading Post

proprietor of the Lake House in Greenville and was co-owner of the steamboat *Ripple*.

In 1908, the Sawyer family and F.E. Gurney of Dover, Maine, formed the Roach River Hotel Trading and Transporting Company, which ran the Kokadjo store and the stage that transported passengers to and from First Roach Pond and Lily Bay.

C.H. Sawyer's postcard of The Roach River House.
Facebook.com/MooseheadMemories/photos

The Sawyers sold out in 1910 to Hollingsworth and Whitney (H&W), which leased the Kokad-Jo Inn (former Roach River House) and farm to Laura and W. Irving Hamilton. Laura managed and cooked for the hotel and became postmaster. A third cottage was added and connected by a veranda and covered platform to the other two cottages and the inn. The Hamiltons leased the inn and store until the 1920s when William Cole and Ralph Turner took over the leases. (In 1930, the Hamiltons purchased the Seboomook House at Northwest Carry and operated it until it burned down in 1945.)[29]

The year-round gravel road from Greenville through Kokadjo to Lily Bay was constructed by the Great Northern Paper Co. in 1919-1920, and comparatively easy year-round access then became available to the Kokad-Jo Inn by stage and motor vehicles.

By 1931, H&W had decided to sell the property and it was purchased by the Hamilton's niece Jess Maddocks Richards and her husband Jack.[30]

In the Maine Woods ad, 1916.

The Great Depression and WWII put an end to the booming business at Kokadjo; the Richards sold the inn, cottages, and property to Herbert and Frances Snow in 1946. The Snows hired staff to run the

Kokad-Jo Inn – Roach River House – Kokadjo Cabins & Trading Post

store and lived at the hotel. Although the cabins were often full, the hotel was not, so the Snow's stopped renting hotel rooms, closed the kitchen, and rented the cottages as housekeeping cabins.

The photo shows the Kokad-Jo Inn buildings and farm, with pulpwood impounded at the First Roach Pond Outlet for sluicing down the Roach River to Moosehead Lake. Once at the lake, the pulpwood was towed in log booms to the east outlet for sluicing down the Kennebec River to paper mills. Such log drives ended in 1976.

maineanencyclopedia.com.

The post office closed in 1966, and Herbert Snow sold-out to Richard Whiting and Don Curtis from Massachusetts. The new owners considered reopening the hotel but found one side of the foundation had collapsed, and the decision was made to keep the hotel building closed. In the 1970s, environmental regulations required the installation of a septic system, and the turn of society toward hiking, recreation, and the popularity of snowmobiling grew. Whiting and Curtis decided to sell, and Robert Berzinis from Penobscot, Maine, and Robert Colarusso became the new owners in 1976. After making needed improvements that included installing a wastewater treatment plant, the two owners sold to George and

Kokad-Jo Inn – Roach River House – Kokadjo Cabins & Trading Post

Linda Midla in 1981. The Midlas operated the sporting camps until 1986, when they sold to Fred and Nick Candeloro, who repaired and remodeled the then 100-year-old camps, changed the name to Kokadjo Camps, and razed the hotel.[31]

The Midlas continued to run the old Kokadjo Country Store on a year-round basis to serve tourists, hunters, fishermen, and snowmobilers. They operated the store until 1992 when Gary Stiles and Wendy Reimen-Schneider tried to keep the store solvent. The site was subject to environmental control standards raised by state land use regulations, however, which required expensive modifications. Additionally, a new Kokadjo Trading Post Store was built across the street by Fred and Nick Candeloro in 1993, which created direct competition.[32]

Former Kokadjo store. maineanencyclopedia.com

The Candeloros bought the old country store from the Midlas, designation as an historic landmark was granted by the state, and the structure is now a private residence.

The Kokadjo Cabins and Trading Post are open 365 days each year and offer a comprehensive array of services and opportunities for visitors. Among the facilities are rental cabins, and a convenience store which stocks groceries, beverages, ice, souvenirs, seasonal outdoor gear, gasoline, motor oil, and emergency parts. Before or

Kokad-Jo Inn – Roach River House – Kokadjo Cabins & Trading Post

after riding the snowmobile trails, fishing, or moose watching, visitors and locals can eat at the full-service restaurant.

Photos from kokadjo.com

For snowmobilers, the trading post and camps are located directly on ITS 85-86 and Route 66, and two trail groomers are operated throughout the season to maintain trails. Snowmobile repair supplies are available at the store, and nonresident snowmobile registrations may be purchased, too. Guided tours can be arranged.

There's also easy access to over 100 miles of marked ATV trails. Nonresident ATV registrations are available at the store, as well as gasoline and other supplies.

The Trading Post is a state-licensed tagging station where hunters can register their big game. Other opportunities for hunters include upland bird and rabbit hunting, and crated hunting dogs are allowed in the cabins. The Roach River chain of ponds continues to provide

Kokad-Jo Inn – Roach River House – Kokadjo Cabins & Trading Post

fantastic trout and salmon fishing. Boats, motors, canoes, and kayaks (2-person) are also available for rent.

For guests with more nature-based interests, activities such as wildlife observation for moose and deer abound. Birdwatching includes loons, bald eagles, ospreys, ducks of all kinds, warblers, and grouse.

Nick and Marie Candeloro have owned and operated the Kokadjo Cabins and Trading Post since 1990.

Lily Bay House

Lily Bay House. The first building on the easterly shore of the lake at Lily Bay and the confluence of North and Lily Bay Brooks, was a logging camp turned "shanty" run by the Hildreth brothers about 1840. The Maine state land agent sold Township A, Range 14 (Lily Bay Township) in 1828 to Samuel A. Bradley, Esquire, of Fryeburg. A series of ownership transactions and a partition agreement in November 1848 resulted in two Hallowell men, Henry Reed and John O. Page owning both the Lily Bay farm and the Hildreth shanty already established there. Reed and Page remained the landowners until April 1856, when they sold to fellow Hallowell townsman Ambrose Merrill. Presumably the Hildreth brothers continued their shanty's operation into the 1850s, but by the end of the decade it would appear they were no longer involved with it. In September 1856, Merrill sold the 160-acre "Lily Bay farm site" (as opposed to the "Hildreth shanty") to Oliver and John Eveleth of Greenville, father and son businessmen and landowners. Osgood Mansell served as proprietor for the Eveleth's Lily Bay farmhouse, and was succeeded by his sons Horace and Charles.[33]

In 1876, the M.G. Shaw Lumber Company purchased the property; and remodelled and enlarged the farmhouse into a hotel with a lobby, kitchen, and dining rooms on the first floor, 20 guest rooms on the second floor, and a men's dormitory on the third. A two-story ell on the back held the staff quarters and laundry.

After the long period of log driving and a steady logging camp diet of baked beans, the woods crews particularly craved a first meal of ham and eggs.

The Shaw Company's intention was to house lumber crews in the spring when roads were muddy and nearly impassable and the lake ice unsafe for wagons. Boats couldn't run, either, because ice hadn't yet left the lake. Large crews came out of the woods and sought rooms with no notice whatsoever. Lumbermen, though, found that instead of staying at the hotel during the spring "break" it was preferable to be in Bangor where boredom was more easily broken. Tempers tended to grow short, too, within the close quarters of the hotel during the time before ice-out.

In the Maine Woods ad, 1905.

Among the proprietors of the hotel during this period of the Shaw's ownership were Dan Wells and his wife, and Henry Tremblay, Charles Ray, Frank L. Gipson, and G.H. Hunt. Alphonso "Phon" Bradeen served there for 22 years. In 1901, proprietor F. L. Gipson's ad promised "Plenty of big fish, healthy pastimes, and the best of accommodations for all comers." Daily passenger and mail connections to and from Greenville were provided by steamboat during open water, and a telephone connection was also available. Guides, canoes, and camping supplies could be obtained at reasonable rates.

The Shaws also established a stage line between Greenville and Lily Bay, and on to Kokadjo at the Roach River (which actually empties into Spencer Bay, north of Lily Bay) for passengers and mail. The stage line provided regular mail to the Lily Bay House, which was a

Lily Bay House

welcome change, since previously mail north and south moved only when someone who was traveling asked guests if they had mail to send. The overland route provided easy access to the Roach River and the Roach Ponds that teemed with fish and wildlife, and the hotel began to attract guests interested in hunting and fishing, and guides arrived to assist them.

The ownership of the hotel altered in 1904 with the Hollingsworth and Whitney Paper Company's (H&W) purchase of the buildings and property to support their pulpwood operations; the 44 cleared acres of the property were used to grow hay for the oxen used in wood harvesting. Proprietors employed by H&W to cater to the sporting trade were Fred Wyman and Sherman Douglass.

GNP Co. leased the Lily Bay House buildings from 1913-1919 to house crews constructing the new 23-mile road to its massive Ripogenus Dam then being constructed on the West Branch of the Penobscot River at Chesuncook Lake. The dam would create the third largest lake in Maine and was said to be one of the five greatest storage basins in the world.

GNP Co. warehouse at upper left and the Lily Bay House at the right, at the mouth of North and Lily Bay Brooks (detail). Collection of The Moosehead Historical Society #1998.13.19.

Lily Bay House

During the building of Ripogenus Dam, much of the heavy construction equipment was hauled across the ice from the Mt. Kineo dock in Rockwood to Lily Bay. GNP Co. built a wharf at Lily Bay and constructed a large adjacent storehouse to handle the quantities of supplies and equipment needed for the Ripogenus Dam project and to support summertime woods operations on the east side of the lake.

By 1919, the Lily Bay House could boast of a completed auto road constructed by GNP Co. from Greenville about 10 miles northerly through Lily Bay.[34]

After the expiration of the GNP Co. lease, H&W leased the hotel to Sam Bigney who operated it from 1931-1942. Bigney seemed to be well-attuned to the times because it became a very popular resort. Correspondence at the Moosehead Historical Society from Robert Gray to a prospective guest on May 26, 1952, described the Lily Bay House and Cabins as having:

> "many attractive bedrooms with comfortable twin beds. Our dining room has gained a reputation for its good, wholesome, food attractively arranged and served in abundance. The rates for the main house are $7.50 per person per day without a bath, or $8.50 with bath. Three meals are included in these rates. We put up pack lunches for guests who prefer to make a day of fishing.
>
> There are two styles of cabins:
>
> No.1: Log-style has living-dining room kitchenette, modern bath with shower, wood stoves for heat, hot and cold running water, electricity, and gas for cooking. All bedding, dishes, cooking utensils, are furnished. The log style cabins rent for $50 a week up to four persons.
>
> No 2: Smaller style cabins with two bedrooms with a double bed in each, kitchen, and chemical toilet adjoining the cabin. All bedding, dishes, cooking utensils, and running water are

provided. All cabins are arranged along the shore. The smaller cabin rate is $35 a week up to four persons. We make baked goods to order for our cabin guests with home made bread a specialty."

In the Maine Woods ad, 1905.

Lily Bay House

By the mid 1950s, a steady drop in Lily Bay House business was caused by both the decline of tourist interest in hotels in such remote locations and by an aging hotel facility. Gray shut down the hotel in 1955, and no one else came forward to lease it. Several of the adjacent cabins were sold, H&W was acquired by the Scott Paper Company in 1954, and the Lily Bay House was then purposely burned to the ground in 1958.

Lily Bay Camps. The Lily Bay Camps appear to have been primarily houskeeping cabins that were becoming popular at the time. They occupied part of the former Lily Bay House site in the 1940s.

Lily Bay Camps in the 1940s. Collection of the author.

Lily Bay Cottages. Where the historic Lily Bay Hotel once stood a century ago, now stand two modern waterfront cottages The cottages are surrounded by water on two sides and four acres of lawn and wildflowers where moose visit often. With vaulted ceilings and plenty of large windows, the cottages provide views out of every window. The knotty pine paneling and comfortable furnishings and amenities provide a rustic retreat without having to rough it. Whatever the season, guests can take full advantage of all the activities that Moosehead Lake and the surrounding region have to offer or can truly just relax and enjoy one of the best views on the lake. Both cottages have large parking areas and share over 1000' of water frontage including a small picnic island, dock, and swim area.

Marr's Indian Pond Camps

Marr's Sporting Camps were located at the head of Indian Pond, where the east and west outlets of Moosehead Lake converge about four miles southwest of Rockwood. Michael Marr, who emigrated from Canada, founded the Indian Pond Camps in 1894, and the photo below shows the camps were fully operational by 1895 on land owned by Elias Milliken. In 1899, Milliken sold Marr 540 acres as the site of Indian Pond Camps.

A small booklet boasted that the people one met at Mike Marr's were the sorts of people one met at home.

Cyrus Goodrich and party at Marr's Camps, Indian Pond, 1895. Cyrus (at left) had a home in Greenville in the 1880s, but eventually moved to the Kennebec, downstream from Wilson's on East Outlet. He ran a successful farm and supplied nearby sporting camps. (G.D. Hamilton) Facebook.com/MooseheadMemories/photo

Marr's Indian Pond Camps

"There are no loud sports here, there are no violently fashionable people ... the men, for the most part are in one or another of the professions, and they bring their wives and children." Marr's offered "all the comforts of home, a clean kitchen, good food, and a quick, quiet, and efficient dining room ... it is not a slapdash hit or miss affair at all. ... All in all, the people who come remain happy and they leave reluctant, determined to come again."

Marr's Camp bell (detail). Collection of The Moosehead.Historical Society #2022.0082.

A well-remembered tradition was the reponsibility of the children to ring the camp bell three times daily to call guests to meals.

As with other sporting camps, the Indian Pond Camps provided mail service to its guests at its own Tarratine Post Office.

In the Maine Woods ad, 1904.

The sporting camp experienced at least two devastating fires, one in 1898 and another in 1941, but was rebuilt after each one.

The Somerset/Rockwood line of the Maine Central Railroad ran close to the camps, and the camps were a "flag stop" where guests could be dropped-off or picked-up without going to the Kineo Station at Rockwood. That changed in 1933, though, when the railroad ceased operation due to competition from the automobile. To adjust, Marr modified his Ford station wagon to add flanged wheels so he could drive the abandoned rail line west to Lake Moxie or east to Rockwood to transport guests. When the rails were removed, he converted the vehicle back to rubber tires.

M. J. MARR'S
Indian Pond Camps
INDIAN POND, MAINE

A SPORTING RESORT OF ESTABLISHED REPUTATION

Deep in the forest, looking out on Squaw Mountain, with a hundred ponds nearby and a big river flowing past, these camps offer a variety of attractions seldom equalled.

INDIAN POND CAMPS represent the result of a quarter of a century's experience with sporting camps. Neatly kept cabins, good beds, efficient service, the best of food and abundance of it, excellent fishing and hunting, and the rigid personal supervision of Mr. Marr combine to keep up the reputation these camps have enjoyed so long.

"A Vacation at Indian Pond is a Vacation Well Spent"

Illustrated Booklet Sent to Any Address on Request to

M. J. MARR - SOMERSET JUNCTION, ME.

Ad from *Vacationland,* a magazine of the Maine Central Railroad, 1927. Maine State Library, Digital Maine, p. 94.

W.S. Bradford served as proprietor in the late 1930s.

Marr's Indian Pond Camps remained in business until 1954, when the site was flooded by the impoundment of the new Harris Station Hydroelectric Dam constructed at the Indian Pond outlet. The dam raised the level of Indian Pond by 20', increasing the surface area from 2 to 5½ square miles.

Maynard's in Maine

Maynard's camps are open year-round and are located one mile from Moosehead Lake on the Moose River.

Maynard's in Maine lodge and two of their 21 cabins. Maynard's Facebook photo.

Camp founder and owner Walter Maynard was an extraordinary man with a huge appetite for adventure and a love for the north woods of Maine. He was a "big game hunter" and enjoyed visiting exotic places such as Guyana (the Cooperative Republic of Guyana), from which he returned with a boa constrictor snakeskin, the pelts of two water tigers (jaguars), and other souvenirs of the jungle.

Born in 1885 in Rutland, Massachusetts, his mother died when he was only eight. Times were hard for the family, and he was sent to live on a farm where he was ill-treated. At the age of nine, he ran away to Boston, and was eventually placed with a family who cared for him well. When he was age ten, he chanced to meet the Maine guide Fred Wilson who was the owner of Wilson's east outlet camps on the lake. Wilson filled his imagination with stories of the north woods as only guides can tell them.

In the early 1900s, Maynard earned Maine Guide license #4316. As a young man, he worked at the Mt. Kineo Resort and there, in 1911, he met Alice Destraz, a young woman from Switzerland. They married in 1913 and bought 50 acres of land from Harry Johnson on the north side of the Moose River, the site of a farm which had been destroyed by fire. They cleared the brush from the land, leaving taller trees to grow. In 1919, Maynard, at age 34, decided to build a sporting camp on the site.

At first named The Firs, the sporting camp was just one cabin built for guests. Five cabins and a barn were then constructed, and two small buildings were moved to the site. Soon there were 31 guests at one time for meals. Daily mail service and long-distance telephone service were provided.

The Firs ad excerpt, *Vacationland* magazine, 1927, Maine Central Railroad, Maine State Library, Digital Maine, p. 94.

It was found that The Firs was also the name of a place in Bar Harbor, so Maynard changed the name to Maynard's Camps in the 1920s, and then to Maynard's in Maine. Unfortunately, Alice died of tuberculosis, but Walter remarried in 1937 to Vivian Hamilton. With Maynard's hard work, success continued with annual growth for the next twelve years. In the late-1930s, there were as many as 42 guides at the camps at one time, one for each guest.

Maynard's Camps

The camps are in the very heart of the Moosehead Lake region. 20 minutes by launch from The Mount Kineo; 3 miles from Kineo Station. Camps are reached by way of Maine Central Railroad, and Bangor & Aroostook Railroad via Greenville Jct. We are 40 miles from Canada, and you can now drive to camp in your car over a good road. 1060 feet above sea level; and hay fever is unknown. There are comfortable beds, home cooking and a generous table. 10 private cabins, accommodating from two to eight persons in each; running water in all of them; some with baths. Spring water, daily mail, garage, telephone and telegraph connections. Salmon, trout and togue fishing. Deer and partridge hunting. In May, June and September some of the very best trout and salmon fishing in the State of Maine can be had directly in front of the camps. 100 ponds and streams can be reached from camp by car or canoe, any of them only a day's trip. Launches, canoes, rowboats and cars for hire. This is a camp where you can bring your family in perfect safety for sport or comfort. Rates $21.00 to $35.00 weekly. References and booklet on request. **WALTER H. MAYNARD**, Rockwood, (Kineo Station) Maine.

In the Maine Woods ad, 1930.

Maynard's in Maine

Railroads first brought sports and visitors to Greenville in the mid-1880s, and they then traveled to the Kineo area by steamboat. With the construction of the Maine Central Railroad's line to Kineo Station in 1906, Maynard's in Maine was just three miles from the rail terminus. In 1927, it became accessible by auto.

The present lodge was constructed in 1928, with the first floor containing a lobby with a piano, library with games, office, and a dining room that seated 50 with a massive fireplace. On the second floor were nine guest rooms.

In the days before electric refrigeration, 1,200 cakes of ice were cut and stored each winter to keep food cool during the coming summer. For winter heat, 100 cords of wood were cut and stacked and 15 tons of coal delivered.

Prior to 1942, Maynard's Camps operated this motor launch for the enjoyment of their guests. A newspaper article reported "Capt. Roger Maynard, who's a pilot, guide, chauffer, cabin boy, painter, electrician, carpenter and generally an all-around man will operate the Camp Launch as usual and will make trips on the Lake by the hour, trip, or day."

Maynard's launch *Tee*. Collection of The Moosehead Historical Society (detail). #2019.76.0011.

Maynard's in Maine

From 1942-1964, Maynard's in Maine operated this 25-passenger vessel for fishermen and camp excursions.

*Moosehead Gazette (*detail), July 29, 1966.
Collection of The Moosehead Historical Society #2017.43.0018.

The camps have grown to 99.9 acres in size. With cabin rentals that vary in size and a family style dining room open for breakfast and dinner, and there are activities for everyone. Twelve out of the thirteen cabin rentals are original to the campground, and most were built by Walter [Maynard] and a few friends and "anyone who could pound a nail straight." The cabin rentals have a rustic charm with the comfort of home; some have kitchens and others are without cooking stoves.

Maynard's Moose River location is just a short 10-minute boat ride to Moosehead Lake. With Maynard's own docks, it is easy to tie up a boat during one's stay. Boats are available for rent, too. If you are dining with them in their dining room, they can fry up your catch for you upon request.

After running Maynard's for 32 years, Walter passed away, leaving his business to his son Roger. Roger would then head Maynard's for 45 years until he, too, passed, leaving Maynard's to his only son William and his wife Gail.

William and Gail began managing the lodge and camps in the 1960s and have been running the business for 53 years now. With the help of their children and grandchildren, Maynard's family ownership and management extends out for six generations.

In 2022, Maynard's Camps turned 103 years old and keeps deep roots in Rockwood.

Maynard's in Maine. Facebook.com page

Miller's Training Camp

One of the best known camps on the lake was Miller's Training Camp on Harford's Point, which was well-liked for fishing and vacations throughout the 1930s. Not a sporting camp in the traditional sense, it was designed by owner Charles Miller to provide physical training to boxers and other sports figures of the day in an outdoor setting. Miller was a natural publicist, a characteristic with which he generated frequent and positive publicity for both the lake and his camp. He became a reasonably well-known boxer and was widely recognized as an outstanding cook.

Maurice Charles Miller was born in Bangor on July 4, 1900. As a young man, he had a brief career as a boxer under the name of "Irish Jack O'Brien," but gave-up the ring after three years of fighting. He moved back into the woods and started work at age 17 in 1917 as a Maine licensed guide for summer visitors. One trip followed another, and Miller's love for the vast wild Moosehead region became increasingly deep as he began to develop his physical fitness theories.

During winters, he went to New York City where he worked as a trainer in an athletic club. On his days off, he loafed around Stillman's Gym where he met some of his future customers.

He was a tireless guide, a crack shot, and expert canoeman. At first he did most of his guiding from the Piscataquis Exchange Hotel in Greenville Junction.

About 1924, Miller advertised his summer school for boys and school of woodcraft, Camp Wapakoneta, which seems to have been a short-term venture.

Miller's Training Camp

```
CAMP WAPAKONETA    (FOR BOYS)    ON MOOSEHEAD LAKE, MAINE
       A summer school for boys and school of woodcraft
   REAL CAMPING TRIPS assisted by Maine Guides.  Send for Booklet to
M. CHARLES MILLER    -    -    GREENVILLE JUNCTION, MAINE
```

In the Maine Woods ad, 1924.

In the Maine Woods ad, 1925.

In 1936, Miller opened a training and conditioning camp for fighters at his camps at Harford's Point on Moosehead's west shore near Greenville.

Miller's Training Camp

**CHARLEY MILLER
The Best Friend
of All Champions**

And Here Is The Reason Why:

I am a registered guide and trainer; I am not a doctor and I do not pretend to be one, my friends call me "Charley". My physical training camps are on Moosehead Lake three miles from Greenville. My purpose is to put men and women into the best possible physical condition. I use no magic, no trick formulas, I use common sense and I get results. That is why I made Jack Dempsey and his wife saw five cords of wood for me last Fall, they still like to keep in condition.

**"DIFFERENT than the REST
... BETTER than the BEST"**

Hedda Liverman of New York with a ten lb. salmon that she caught with Charley Miller

For further information write to:
CHARLEY MILLER   Moosehead Lake, Greenville, Me.

Collection of The Moosehead Historical Society #2016.10.0009.

Bangor Daily News outdoors columnist Bill Geagan wrote the following history about Charley Miller in his "On the Trail" column in February 1965, titled: "As Boxer, Guide and Cook Has Made Many A Headline For Moosehead."

> "In the summer of 1916, a husky newsboy stepped from a Bangor & Aroostook passenger train at Greenville Junction. He gazed in awe for the first time at the majestic Moosehead Lake and its forested mountains, loved what he saw, and from there went on to devote most of his life to singing the praises of the region far and wide across the land. Charley Miller of Bangor was only 16 years old at the time. On his new job he had sold newspapers, magazines, cigars, cigarettes, candy, and fruit on the train's daily run to that then bustling village on the tail of the big lake.

Miller's Training Camp

And he has, through his personal efforts, brought to the big lake numerous celebrities in sports and the other professions. For instance, from his beloved world of boxing there were Benny Leonard, Jack Dempsey, Jack Sharkey, Gene Tunney, Al McCoy, Jess Willard, Jack Johnson, Joe Lynch, and many others including Primo Carnera. Charley brought Carnera and his entire staff from New York to Moosehead Lake for weeks of preliminary training in advance of his defense of his world championship in March of 1934. Newspapers and the radio chains from all the country carried repeated reports on such visits and events. (Carnera reigned as the boxing World Heavyweight Champion from June 29, 1933, to June 14, 1934, when Max Baer defeated him).

Another stunt that brought widespread publicity to the land of the big lake was walking on snowshoes from Seboomook to Greenville Junction to the train and New York to accept the invitation of his friend Jack Dempsey to attend the official opening of the latter's new restaurant. Charlie made sure that the newspapers' press services and radio hookups knew about it, and they ate it up.

He got even more publicity for the Moosehead region when, with the words, 'Moosehead Lake' lettered large on his shirt back, he walked the 250 miles on snowshoes from Bangor to appear and perform at the New England Sportsmen's show in Boston. It was the same publicity-minded Charley who made arrangements for news reel cameramen to come to Harford's Point to cover the start of his two-man back to Nature stunt. The movies of the young 'Tarzans' were shown all over the country. And the newspapers and radios clamored for daily reports.

Yet another of Charley's publicity stunts is to challenge the Red Sox slugger Ted Williams to a fly casting contest. Ted, he said, was a distance caster, but he figured when it came to accuracy he could outcast Ted. The proposal was made for the Boston Sportsmen Show and the target was a fifty cent piece put in a water tank with each contestant to have ten casts. It is not known whether the contest took place, but the idea lends insight to the promotional minds of folks like Miller. The billing and anticipation would be enough to attract showgoers

In his many appearances at Sportsmen Shows from Bangor over this state and on into others, as far as Ohio, Charley was always 'The Guide from Moosehead Lake, Maine.' And when he matched his canoemanship against the rowing ability of Steve Crusher Casey, world's champion sculler on the Charles River in Boston, he was again carrying his banner of the region he loved.

Charley and his beloved Moosehead Lake country have been headlined copy over these many years as he prepared thousands of meals over the guide's wood fires at outdoor shows, fairs, conventions, institutions, schools, orphanages, Scout camps, boys' and girls' camps, public exhibitions, and important cooking contests, too."

Other newspaper clippings add that Babe Ruth, Joe Louis, Ted Williams, Arthur Godrey, Bing Crosby, and Bob Hope were among the friends and acquaintances that he guided and hosted.

Miller became one of a small handful of Maine Sportsmen who appeared in advertisements in sporting magazines, as well as *Life* magazine, promoting products such as SOS scouring pads, Eveready batteries, and Camel cigarettes.

In 1963, he founded the Charley Miller Outdoor Cooker Corporation to market his all-purpose outdoor cooker, a kind of reflective oven. Such ovens captured heat from a campfire to bake pies and biscuits; baking items evenly with a reflector oven often taxed the cooking skills of guides.

Miller's Training Camp

Bangor Daily News, February 1965.

Miller's Training Camp

Maine guide Charley Miller assists boxer Jack Dempsey adjust one of his snowshoes while Dempsey smokes a cigar. Image courtesy of Special Collections, Raymond H. Fogler Library, DigitalCommons@UMaine.

The Raymond H. Fogler Library at the University of Maine contains a collection of papers and photographs of Charley Miller's life and exploits, as well as a group of 16 mm films and a number of scrapbooks and notebook that he compiled. He once owned the largest collection of fight films in the country. These collections document his career as a young boxer, an energetic guide, a greatly-admired outdoor cook, and an inveterate promoter.

Mt. Kineo Hotel and Resort

No other hotels or camps in the Moosehead area could match the elegance of the Mt. Kineo Hotel and Resort.

Situated on a peninsula in Moosehead Lake, the Mt. Kineo House site was spectacular. Mt. Kineo (comprised of flint, hence the Abenaki name "Kineo") juts out from the east side of the lake and is about 800' high with sheer 700' - 800' cliffs on its easterly face.

Once the largest hotel on any inland waterway in America, the Mt. Kineo House was first reached by stagecoaches, and later by trains from either Skowhegan to Kineo Station at Rockwood with a one-mile boat shuttle from Rockwood. Alternatively, a train from Newport, Maine, to Greenville with a several hour boat trip by steamer would bring clientele to the resort.

John Bradbury of Bangor, Maine, purchased the Mt. Kineo peninsula and 1,150 acres of land from state of Maine Land Agent Rufus McIntire for $325 in 1840. The first development there was a small log tavern, or "public house," built by brothers William and Henry Hildreth in 1844 with overnight accommodations for a few people who were in the area to fish, hunt, or work in lumbering. H.G.O. Barrows served as manager for many years.

The "first" Mt. Kineo House was built in 1848 by Capt. Joshua Fogg. Improvements were continually made to the structure until it became a 40-room, two and one-half-story hotel with a porch overlooking the lake. By 1856, it was owned by Winthrop L. Chenery of Watertown, Massachusetts, and managed initially by John Crocker. In 1868 Orrin A. Dennen of Shirley, Maine, became the proprietor.

Mt. Kineo Hotel and Resort

The "first" Mt. Kineo House, 1848-1868. Ricker Hotel Co. photo from www.baharris.org. Brian Harris website posting of February 24, 2004.

The "second" Mt. Kineo House (detail) 1868 *The Northern* magazine, May 1922.

During 1868-1871 while a new hotel was being built, guests were entertained and lodged in tents and an outbuilding that was formerly a bowling alley. A spruce-bark lodge served as dining room and kitchen.

Mt. Kineo Hotel and Resort

The expanded second Mt. Kineo House (detail), now called the "third." circa 1871-1882. Collection of The Moosehead Historical Society #98.22.08.

The 1871-1882 "third" Mt. Kineo House with additions constructed in 1880 and 1881. It was destroyed by fire in 1882, along with an 1876 annex and boat house.

Excerpt from poster in the Camp Caribou main lodge of the "fourth" Mt. Kineo Hotel ca 1884. Roy Finch collection.

The hotel was then rebuilt in 1884 as the "fourth" structure. The Mt. Kineo House was reconstructed in grand style with 200 guest rooms, and a dining room which could seat 500. Amenities included steam heat, gas and electric lights, hot and cold running water, a steam-

Mt. Kineo Hotel and Resort

operated elevator, electric bells, telephone, telegraph, and daily mail delivery. It also held a bowling alley and an ornate ballroom. . .

Visitors enjoyed walking trails, and fishing and hunting with expert local guides who were hired for the season. Activities on the resort's grounds included golfing on the 9-hole "Northwood Ho!" golf course, tennis, archery, baseball teams, horseback riding, croquet, concerts, and movies twice each week. The resort owned and operated steam yachts for daily outings: *Day Dream*, *Kineo*, and *George A*. Resort watercraft, such as *The Patsy*, provided fast transportation between Kineo and the train stations about 20 miles south in Greenville.

A separate guides house was constructed to accommodate the dozens of Maine guides hired to escort the "sports" for fishing and hunting. Other outbuildings included an annex, store, and stable, and sawmill.

Orrin A. DePaul retired as manager in 1900 after 32 years of service and was succeeded by Charles Judkins.

The Patsy. Facebook.com/MooseheadMemories/photos

The Somerset Railroad extended the rail line to Moosehead Lake in 1906 to serve Mt. Kineo House resort hotel and other resorts and

Mt. Kineo Hotel and Resort

sporting camps at Moosehead Lake. Hotel patrons arrived via an overnight trip in Pullman cars from large eastern cities and reached the Mt. Kineo hotel by a steamboat shuttle from the railroad terminal at Kineo Station. The train had plush upholstered coaches, baggage cars, and combination smoking-baggage cars with leather seats.

The Maine Central Railroad (MCRR) purchased the Somerset Railway in 1911, and the railway became known as the Kineo branch of the MCRR. The Mt. Kineo Hotel and Resort was also purchased by the Maine Central and was managed by the Ricker Hotel Co. (which also owned the Samoset Resort in Rockport and the Poland Spring House and Resort).

Fresh vegetables were available daily from the hotel's 350-acre Deerhead Farm on the lake shoreline about four miles north of the resort. The farm also provided hay for the farm animals and the resort's riding horses. A gravel road connected the farm with the Kineo resort.

Deerhead Farm. ca. 1911. Facebook.com/Moosehead Memories/photos

Mt. Kineo Hotel and Resort

In 1911, the Kineo Hotel saw a radical makeover. New construction included a wing five-stories high, a fireproof kitchen, and 50 private baths. The former steam operated elevator was replaced by two hydraulic lifts. Other additions included a boathouse, a long pier for steamers and yachts, and new dormitory for the "help."

Bigger   **Completely**

New Mt. Kineo House

Better   **Modernized**

On the Shore of 40-Miles-Long Moosehead Lake

Every recurring year has seen this famous recreation rendezvous improved here and there, as occasion demanded. Now an elaborate and radical plan of improvements has been carried out, whereby we gain 75 new rooms with baths, a large addition to our dining room, a completely fireproof kitchen, new electric and boiler plants, and other modernizing changes. All these improvements mean a bigger, better vacation home for YOU in this great natural playground. Better plan early for a Kineo outing; "it's the thing to do."

SPORTSMEN should remember that we furnish guides, camping outfits and supplies.

The best sport of Maine woods and waters is to be had at Kineo and vicinity — finest of moose, deer and bear hunting; America's record quantity and quality fishing for trout, togue and landlocked salmon; superb canoe trips; motor boating, sailing, golf, mountain climbing, etc. Kineo, good times and good health are an inseparable trio—as any of our former guests will tell you. Unsurpassed hotel service and cuisine; everything just to YOUR liking. Handsome descriptive booklet sent on request.

C. A. JUDKINS, Manager,
KINEO, MAINE

In the Maine Woods ad, 1911.

By 1917, in the "fifth" iteration of Mt. Kineo Hotel, there were accommodations for 500 guests who could enjoy a view from each room, rely on a well-known New York staff physician for medical care, drink medicinal water, and experience daily music concerts.

Mt. Kineo Hotel and Resort

Rooms cost $4.00 a night in-season and direct transportation from Boston with a splendid buffet offered for $15.00.

The "fifth" and most grand of the Mt. Kineo hotels, ca 1911-33 (detail). Known as "The New Mt. Kineo Hotel," it included the Breakwater sporting club (in foreground) and the long breakwater. Collection of The Moosehead Historical Society #19954.63.

Railroad traffic to Kineo Station at the Rockwood landing ceased operating by the early 1930s. By then, the era of summer-long residency at grand hotels had all but disappeared due to growing public appetites for the newly emerging travel by automobile and Great Depression that lasted until 1938.

In 1938, a federal antitrust case caused the discontinuation of government subsidies to mail-carrying railroads that owned other businesses, and this led to MCRR's decision to sell the entire property with the condition that the hotel be demolished because it had fallen into disrepair.

Local entrepreneur Louis Oakes purchased the property and complied with the sale condition of razing the then 425-room main

Mt. Kineo Hotel and Resort

hotel. Much of the interior contents, including plumbing, had been removed before a 1938 fire destroyed the hotel structure.

A smaller-scale hotel accommodating 120 guests was built on the site in 1937, but WWII forced cancellation of any further redevelopment plans.

Early in the post-World War II years, an underwater cable brought electricity to Kineo, a new 36-room hotel was built, and the golf course was re-designed to be a 13-hole facility. Yet the hotel still struggled. In the 1950s, C. Max Hilton and his wife Edith, daughter of Louis Oakes, invested in the hotel and over the next 20 years sought to revive it as an American Plan resort.

By the late-1950s, the Mt. Kineo Hotel gradually ceased to exist as it went through a series of sales and ownerships that attempted to revive it. In 1966, it was sold to the Rockwood-Kineo Corporation and the 1937 Annex was branded as a Treadway Inn by R.H. Rines and H.A. Atherton until 1969.

Postcard detail from Facebook.com/MooseheadMemories/photos

Mt. Kineo Hotel and Resort

Treadway Inn 1966-1969. This postcard shows the peninsula after the removal of the Mt. Kineo Hotel and the other buildings on the site. Remaining are the yellow resort staff dormitory at the center, to the right of that is the 120 room Annex built in 1937 which became the Treadway Inn, and the Breakwater Sporting Club/Moosehead Lake Yacht Club at the right. "Cottage Row" is at the left. Collection of the author.

In 1971, the property and remaining buildings were sold again. By 1980, the mortgage came into default and the hotel put up for auction. Another attempt to make it a going concern was conceived in 1986, but the multi-million-dollar plan never came to fruition. In 1996, the Annex was demolished, and in 2016, the old dormitory for resort staff, the last hotel-related building on the site, was dismantled and burned.

The halcyon days of the Mt. Kineo Hotel lasted more than a century, with its most successful years occurring between 1883 and 1930. It employed many local residents and was a symbol of American entrepreneurial wealth and stability prior to World War II.[35]

Still existing to this day, however, are seven turn-of-the-last century cottages in "Cottage Row" along the former Kineo Resort's shoreline facing Rockwood. They were built by the Ricker Hotel Co.

between 1901 and 1912 and are now privately-owned. They were nominated and have been included on the National Register of Historic Places which describes them as follows:

Alpen Cottage. Alpen Cottage was built in 1904 and may be a design of the Lewiston, Maine, architectural firm Coombs and Gibbs. It has a gambrel roof, and its porch is partially exterior and partially engaged, with Tuscan columns supporting the overhanging second story on that portion.

Birch Cottage. Built between 1905 and 1907, this building is a near replica of Fir Cottage, differing only in some details on the tower. Its interior has been altered to expose the interior truss system from which its second floor is suspended, enabling it to have a large living room without posts.

Dogwood Cottage. Dogwood Cottage, built sometime between 1901 and 1904, is essentially Dutch Colonial Revival in design, with a shingled exterior and shingle style details. It has an engaged porch (giving the second floor more square footage), with turned posts and balusters in the Queen Anne style.

From left to right the cottages shown are: Alpen Cottage, Birch Cottage, Oak Lodge, and Cedar Cottage.

Facebook.com/Moosehead Memories/photos

Mt. Kineo Hotel and Resort

Oak Lodge. Oak Lodge, built in 1912 on the site of a former sporting clubhouse, was the last of the seven to be built and is the only one designed as a duplex. Its design has a distinct Craftsman flavor with ribbon windows and exposed rafter tails. The building's two units are mirror images and have been at times combined into a single dwelling unit. It was known as the Kineo House Inn 1996-2001 and now is privately owned, but its 8,000 square feet of space and nine bedrooms can be rented for weddings and other events.

Cedar Cottage. Cedar Cottage is similar in exterior styling to Dogwood, as a Dutch Colonial with shingle features and an interior layout that is nearly identical to that of Fir Cottage. Architects Coombs and Gibbs may have designed it, or it may merely have been built on altered plans.

Elm Cottage. Elm Cottage was built in 1905 and altered in 1912. Originally L-shaped in plan, its tower was added in 1912 and the angle of the L was enclosed. Unlike most of the other cottages, it is predominantly finished in clapboards instead of shingles.

Fir Cottage. Fir Cottage was built in 1901, and its design is unambiguously attributable to the architectural firm of Coombs and Gibbs. Because of its position at the far north of the row on a sloping lot, it stands at a higher elevation than the other cottages.

The Breakwater Sporting Club. The historic Breakwater building also remains, built as a sporting lodge and yacht club on the resort's waterfront in 1909. It is an architecturally sophisticated example of a sporting lodge, exhibiting Shingle style and Italianate features. Designed by Howard G. Chamberlain, a New York City architect, with funding from the nearby Mount Kineo Resort and the Moosehead Yacht Club, it was one of the centerpieces of the summer resort. Although The Breakwater sat vacant for many years, it underwent restoration in 1999 and was listed on the National Register of Historic Places in 2002. (see also the Private Sporting Clubs chapter).

Mt. Kineo Hotel and Resort

1909 photo (detail) of Breakwater Sporting Club/Moosehead Lake Yacht Club (at left), at the Mt. Kineo Hotel and Resort. Collection of The Moosehead Historical Society #1998.0193.

Thousands of visitors still play the 9-hole golf course annually, accessed by crossing one-mile of Moosehead Lake waters from Rockwood aboard the Kineo Shuttle. The 360° views from the top of Mt. Kineo continue to attract many hikers, a testament to the spectacular landscape that brought visitors to the Kineo Hotel during its heyday. Although the southerly side of the Mt. Kineo peninsula remains privately owned, the northerly portion with its hiking trails is 800-acre state park managed by the Maine Bureau of Parks and Lands.

Northern Pride Lodge

Greenville's Louis Oakes family built the original lodge in 1896 on a five-acre leased lot from the Hollingsworth and Whitney (H&W) lumber company with 550' of shoreline frontage on First Roach Pond, a pristine lake nearly seven miles long. In 1932, Louis Oakes (a surveyor for H&W) and his daughter Edith Hilton purchased the land from H&W and built a cottage, but the property received very little use by the family. The windows were boarded up, and the site became overgrown with brush and trees.

Known locally as the "Oakes Cottage," it remained privately-owned for about the next 100 years. As a youngster in the 1920s, local resident recalled John Dyer delivered eggs to the summer tenants the Kinsman (or Kinsmen) family.

In 1973, John and Frances Richards purchased the cottage and 6.5-acre property and spent many summers there. They sold it to Ken and Rita Trask in 1993, who turned it into a lodge and restaurant, built some campsites, and called it the First Roach Lodge and Campground. The hundreds of thousands of acres of north Maine woods that surrounded it can offer the full range of vacation and recreational experiences.

On February 5, 1987, Melton Sales and Services, Inc. of Bordentown, New Jersey, bought the lodge and property, resold it to John and Nadine Melton the same day, who then resold again that day to Randal and Colleen Richard.

Paul and Georgette Wade purchased the property later in 1987, changed the name to Northern Pride Lodge, and ran it as a small outfitter business offering deer and bear hunting and fishing trips.

The business was purchased from the Wades by Jeff and Barbara Lucas in 1991, who added hot showers for campers. The lodge was

Northern Pride Lodge

uniquely furnished in a semi-Victorian antique-Maine outdoor decor.

Since 2000, Barbara and Wayne Plummer, who met at Lisbon High School, have owned and operated the Northern Pride Lodge, hosting and guiding hunters and anglers.[36]

Room rates include a hearty Maine woods breakfast. An American option includes a boxed lunch and dinner in the dining room or individual meals can be purchased.

Fine dining is also provided for guests, as well as the public by reservation. The lodge's five cozy and comfortable guest rooms accommodate singles, couples, families, or groups. For large parties of eight or more with a minimum three-day stay, guests can reserve the lodge for exclusive use by one group only.

About 15 tenting sites are available, too, and camper trailers and motorhomes are welcome. Electric hookups are an option for campers, drinking water is available, and hot showers and pit toilets are provided. A boat launch ramp adjoins the campground, which makes for easy launching and loading, and docking space is available.

Northern Pride Lodge and Camps. 2021 real estate sales photo.

Northern Pride Lodge

Northern Pride Lodge is surrounded by mountain ponds. Excellent fishing is right at hand, and the camp's Registered Master Maine Guide Wayne Plummer knows the area well. All the needed equipment is provided, or guests can bring their own gear.

Northern Pride Lodge is located in the heart of "Hikers Paradise." The area offers many hiking trips ranging in difficulty that will provide a challenging day to all skill levels. Breathtaking views and abundant wildlife are only a few of the rewards awaiting the ambitious hiker. Two types of moose watching adventures are available, one of which is a scenic trip across First Roach Pond by motorboat, where guests are then offloaded into canoes and/or kayaks. The other option, depending on skill and comfort levels, is for guests to either paddle their own canoe or let the guide get them through to the quiet waters.

Drift boat fishing. Northern Pride Lodge and Campgrounds photo.

Drift boat fishing trips are comfortable, fun, and productive. There's no wading in fast currents on slippery rocks; clients are securely seated or standing supported by thigh braces as the Master Maine Guide expertly positions them for optimal casting and landing fish. His knowledge of the river and oarsmanship keeps putting guests onto fish that are beyond the reach of wading fishermen, particular spots that have proven to hold good fish on many past trips and those that are promising given the varying conditions of the river each day. After a few casts or a hookup, Plummer will let the drift boat ride the current to another riffle, current seam, pool, or protected pocket and reposition fishermen and fisherwomen to best present their fly, often to a visible fish. This is the most productive way to explore Maine's best rivers.

Hunts for bear, deer, and moose are fully supported by the Northern Pride facility, as are small game and game-bird hunting. The camp's location gives ready access to nearly endless hunting territory.

For those seeking a closer encounter for the up-close moose photos in a picturesque setting, canoe trips are available to remote ponds and flowages. Whichever tour clients choose, they should see many moose, and often loons, deer, and bald eagles. The best time of year for moose sightings in and around the water is the first of June through August, with morning and evening tours by reservation.

The adjacent thousands of acres of paper company woodlands contain numerous trails and dirt roads which provide miles and miles of riding for the mountain bike enthusiast. The wide variety of roads and trails range from graded and maintained main roads to overgrown trails that seriously challenge riding skills.[37]

The Moosehead Lake area is a great destination for birders, with vireos and warblers of all sorts and species not found in more southern climes. The hosts can suggest areas that will allow visitors to add some of those elusive birds to their life lists. Boreal chickadees, Bicknell's thrush, spruce grouse, and Canada jays (also known as the 'gorbie') are all residents at some point throughout the year. Bald eagles, loons, pileated woodpeckers, bitterns, and many others are some of the more sought-after species. There are water birds, species that favor the thick evergreen forests, and migratory species of all kinds. No matter the time of year, there are always many birds to lure visitors into the great outdoors.

The lodge and campground were listed for sale by the Plummers in 2021.

Northeast Carry - The Penobscot Hotel

Wood harvesting operations along the lower reaches of the West Branch of the Penobscot River near the towns of Medway, East Millinocket, and Millinocket, began a westward progression up the West Branch in 1825, at first for white pine. Because the white pine had largely disappeared by 1850, the Bangor mills started to accept Penobscot River spruce sawlogs in the 1840s. Moosehead's east and west outlet dams were completed about 1835, and steamboat services also became available on the lake about that time.

It was clear that access to the West Branch from Moosehead Lake at Northeast Carry would become a major route for loggers, because the two destinations were only about 2½ miles apart. In 1846, a group of ten investors received a charter from the Maine State Legislature to construct a land transportation link between the lake at Northeast Carry and the West Branch. Major Bigney was hired to construct an "ox cart railway" of wooden rails connecting the two bodies of water for moving logging supplies and equipment, and to transport people, food, and gear for extended wilderness trips. The lake elevation was 1,027' and the West Branch elevation was about 1,000' with a height of land between of 1091', which allowed for a relatively flat route. The cart, pulled by one or two oxen, could carry two tons and often made four trips per day.

Samuel Hinckley, who lived on the West Branch end of the carry, was the ox cart driver from 1847 to 1850. When he died, he was succeeded by his son.

The use of the wooden railway diminished after about 1860 and it burned in 1863. It was not rebuilt because a substantial tote road had been constructed to serve the route. Also, lumbermen were bringing in their own oxen to support logging operations. Another reason might have been that a single cart making four trips a day was no longer sufficient to meet the needs of the increasing number of loggers.[38]

Ox cart railway illustration from Farrar's *Moosehead Lake, North Woods Wilderness*, 1884.

Loggers continued to use the carry for access to and from the West Branch, and they were increasingly joined by sports traveling to destinations accessed from the West Branch.

By about 1871, George Luce owned both the farm at the Moosehead Lake end of the carry and the Penobscot Hotel on the West Branch at the terminus of the railway.

Wagons replaced the ox cart railway.
Facebook.com/MooseheadMemories/photos

Northeast Carry – The Penobscot Hotel & Trading Company

The Morris farm at the West Branch (north) end of the carry, operated by Joseph Morris, offered traveler services beginning in 1871.

Luce, who also purchased the Winnegarnock House property and buildings on Moosehead Lake at Northeast Carry from Dora Savage in 1891, formed the Moosehead Trading and Transportation Company in 1900 and built the Penobscot Hotel on the West Branch.

In the Maine Woods ad, 1901.

A 1902 fire destroyed his new "Penobscot Hotel" (also called the Moosehead Inn for a period of time), but Luce continued to offer lodging there at the Penobscot "House."

Northeast Carry - Winnegarnock House & Supply Store - Raymond's Country Store

It is unclear when the buildings for lodging and supplies were first built and occupied at Moosehead Lake's Northeast Carry, but by 1872 the landing area was owned by John Appleton and John Ross. A small barn known as Page's Tavern was established there and storage buildings were also present on the site. Nicholas T. Curran operated the Carry House, a two and one-half story house/hotel with an ell on one side.

Simeon and Dora Savage, who had previously managed the Lake House in Greenville, bought Ross' 600 acres of land in 1878 and took over the Carry House, renaming it the Winnegarnock House. They made significant upgrades to attract sportsmen, including doubling the size of the dining room, and finishing more rooms to increase its capacity to 20-25 people. Other amenities included a "piazza" on the lakeside of the hotel, a croquet court, bathhouse, and bowling alley. Carriage rides and horse riding were available, along with canoe and boat rental. Dora Savage played the piano and accompanied singers at small concerts.

With the death of Simeon, in 1891 Dora sold her land and buildings to George Luce, who formed the Moosehead Trading and Transportation Company in 1900. Fred Davis became the proprietor of the buildings in 1901.

Northeast Carry – Winnegarnock House and Supply Store – Raymond's Country Store

Facebook.com/MooseheadMemories/photos

Although a 1902 fire destroyed Luce's new "Penobscot Hotel" built on the West Branch end of the carry, he continued to offer lodging there at the existing Penobscot "House."

Luce built the new Penobscot Hotel on Moosehead Lake at Northeast Carry in 1902 to replace the former Penobscot Hotel on the West Branch end of the carry that had burned. The new hotel was built under a new company named Penobscot Hotel and Trading Company. Frank Gipson was hired as its proprietor, and also managed the Winnegarnock House. Services to hikers, fishermen and hunters continued to be a significant source of activity for the two hotels.

Working through his Penobscot Hotel and Trading Company, Luce's store at Northeast Carry handled the supplies for nearly every logging outfit using the carry as an access point to the north woods.

Luce sold the Penobscot Hotel and Trading Company to Arthur A. Crafts in 1907.

(Readers should be alerted at this point that the name and location of "Penobscot Hotel" can be confusing. Although the name was originally used for Luce's West Branch lodging, he gave the same

Northeast Carry – Winnegarnock House and Supply Store – Raymond's Country Store

name to the new hotel he built at <u>Northeast</u> Carry in 1902 next to the Winnegarnock House.)

. TOURISTS .

Going down the Penobscot, Allegash, or St. John Rivers,

OR TO ANY OF THE

Pleasure Grounds of Northeastern Maine,

will find good hotel accommodation
at either end of the

NORTHEAST CARRY,

MOOSEHEAD LAKE.

During the Summer Season several steamers touch at the CARRY daily. Within gunshot of the Penobscot House flows the west branch of the Penobscot, with its miles of canoeable waters, and near at hand are the beauties of

LOBSTER LAKE.

United States Post-Office at the Carry.

CANOES HAULED PROMPTLY ACROSS THE CARRY;
ALSO TO RUSSELL POND.

FREE CARRIAGE FOR ALL GUESTS OF EITHER HOUSE.

GEORGE C. LUCE . . PROPRIETOR,
WINNEGARNOCK AND PENOBSCOT HOUSES.

Hubbard, Lucius L., *Hubbard's Guide to Moosehead Lake and Northern Maine*, Fifth Edition, revised and enlarged edition of "Summer vacations at Moosehead Lake and Vicinity," published by the author, Cambridge, Massachusetts, 1893.

Crafts hired Thomas B. and Edith Snow as Winnegarnock managers. He also placed under Snow's management the outfitting store that sold all necessary supplies for voyages through the vast northern waters and forests. When clients stepped off the steamer at Northeast

Northeast Carry – Winnegarnock House and Supply Store – Raymond's Country Store

Carry, they would find everything in readiness for the start of the next day. Guides, canoes, and supplies would be in waiting for the jaunt across the carry to the shore of the Penobscot River's West Branch.[39]

Several separate cabins and a large central camp for dancing and socials were built in connection with the Winnegarnock House, and often sporting parties spend a few days there before getting away on the canoe trips.

Prominent among the trips going into the great north woods from Northeast Carry were the 118-mile trip along the East Branch of the Penobscot, the 203-mile Allagash River trip, the 99-mile Allagash Lake trip, and the 27-mile Pine Ponds trip.

Northeast Carry – Winnegarnock House and Supply Store – Raymond's Country Store

THE GATEWAY TO THE HAPPY HUNTING GROUNDS

WINNEGARNOCK HOUSE
Northeast Carry

NORTHEAST CARRY! Doesn't the name bring to your mind visions of brawny guides and canoes with duffle and paddles and setting poles lashed in them? If it doesn't, then it is time you came up to see us and learn how it feels to be on the threshold of the "Great Beyond," that great beyond of the Maine wilderness where, "the red gods call us out and we must go." Every year hundreds of canoeists start from our door over the short carry to the Penobscot West Branch from whence start the canoe trips down the West Branch, East Branch, Allagash and St. John Rivers.

It is a delightful sail up Moosehead Lake on the steamer to our door, with a vista of lake, forest and scores of mountains spread out on every side. Our table offers you the trout fresh from the lake, vegetables fresh from our garden, milk and cream and everything to make the inner man happy. At our door is some of the best trout and togue fishing in the world. Moose and Deer are seen drinking in the lake every day in summer and our guests often see them from their windows. Four miles away is Lobster Lake, one of the most beautiful bodies of water in Maine and fine fishing. Farther off are other famous regions, like Russell Pond, peerless among all hunting-grounds. Our large supply store offers you everything you want to use or wear in the woods. Canoes and guides too are ready at your service.

Write to find out about some more of our good things. Let us send you some of the recommendations from those who know us well. We are proud of them. Look at pages 31 and 73 of this book for views taken at Northeast Carry.

T. B. SNOW

Winnegarnock House   Northeast Carry, Maine

In the Maine Woods ad, 1911.

Northeast Carry – Winnegarnock House and Supply Store – Raymond's Country Store

A FULL HAND IN THE "GAME"

You know what it means to "Paddle your own canoe" down the River of Life, but get a guide to paddle you down the West Branch of the Penobscot, on the Allegash trip and get a new idea of living.

North East Carry, at the head of Moosehead Lake, is the starting point of this world's famous trip through the Maine Woods by its natural waterways.

It is the camp life for those in search of rest and health.

Campers' supplies of every description in the store near the Hotel, canoes and tents to sell or let. Guides who are skillful canoemen and cooks, may be hired by the day or trip.

Sporting Camps connected with the Hotel, situated on the shore of the Lake, make this an ideal summer resort, where fishing and hunting are unexcelled. Write for details, booklet, rates, etc.

"THE WINNEGARNOCK" T. B. SNOW North East Carry, Maine

In the Maine Woods ad, 1914.

Northeast Carry – Winnegarnock House and Supply Store – Raymond's Country Store

The long, wooden, wharf at Northeast Carry was necessary due to the shallow lake depths there. First built in about 1872 and extending approximately 500' into the lake, its length was increased to about 1,000' over the next 20 years to reach enough depth for larger steamboats to dock. It became structurally unsafe, and was removed in 1924 by GNP Co. By then, the company had moved its transportation network around the lake to land-based routes.

The photograph in the ad shows the assemblage of buildings at Northeast Carry in the early 1920s: the wharf is at the far left in front of the warehouses, to the right of the warehouses in the Penobscot Hotel, in the center is the Winnegarnock House, and on the right are rental cabins.

T.B. Snow died in 1921, and his wife Edith continued to manage the Winnegarnock. She was also postmistress until 1924, when she closed the hotel. Later in that same year, Arthur Crafts sold the Northeast Carry property and buildings to GNP Co.

Due to the unsafe conditions of some of the buildings at the carry, in 1925 GNP Co. crews tore down the Winnegarnock House, the dance hall, and the wharf, and did not replace them.

It appears that, in the 1930s, the store was moved into the Penobscot Hotel; in 1939, the Penobscot Hotel's name was changed again, that time to the Northeast Carry Inn.

Northeast Carry – Winnegarnock House and Supply Store – Raymond's Country Store

Northeast Carry—Moosehead Lake
IS A
RESORT OF NATIONAL FAME

FOR CANOEISTS

Northeast Carry is the starting point for the famous Allagash and West Branch canoe trips. We make all arrangements for these trips. Write us and we'll have guides, canoes, camping outfit and provisions ready for the day you designate.

FOR THE SPORTSMEN

Northeast Carry is in the center of one of the biggest fish and game sections of the Maine woods. Besides Moosehead Lake, nearby are Lobster Lake, Russell Stream and numerous other fishing waters. If you want good deer hunting, come to Northeast Carry.

Seboomook Lodge, three miles up the picturesque West Branch by canoe or motor boat, is an attractive spot for private parties. Comfortable sleeping camps and a kitchen camp ready to use.

FOR THE VACATIONIST

Men and women seeking a delightful resort for their vacation can find no more attractive spot than Northeast Carry. Exceptionally good table, separate cabins, a central assembly cabin and up-to-date service are some of the attractions offered in addition to the natural charms of the Northeast Carry country.

For recreation is a dancing pavilion, tennis court, croquet, and a fine beach for swimming and bathing in front of the cabins.

OUR BOOKLET GIVES FULL INFORMATION

THE WINNEGARNOCK, Northeast Carry, Maine
MRS. T. B. SNOW, Manager

In the Maine Woods ad, 1923.

Although there was a succession of owners from the 1930s through the 1960s, the 1939 land lease from GNP Co. at Northeast Carry

Northeast Carry – Winnegarnock House and Supply Store – Raymond's Country Store

included only the Penobscot Hotel built by Luce and some rental cabins just east of the hotel. Its name was changed again, this time to the Northeast Carry Inn and Cabins. W.T. LaCrosse managed the Northeast Carry Inn and Cabins from the 1940s and through at least 1953.

Ed Raymond, Sr. held a GNP Co. lease for a simple camp structure not connected to the inn or cabins in 1954, Ed Raymond, Jr. and Shirley Raymond took over the lease from Ed, Sr. in 1978, and later purchased the seven-acre property.

Ed and Shirley Raymond had come from Attleboro, Massachusetts, to make Northeast Carry their home, and they were the sole year-round residents of Northeast Carry. After several years of experimenting with camp maintenance and propane gas delivery to camps along the lakeshore, and other ideas for establishing feasible businesses for themselves, they decided to expand Ed, Sr.'s camp into Raymond's Country Store. The Raymond's store expansion and some rental cabins were built by the Raymonds without any loans.

The summertime outdoor sports portions of their business declined, however, partly due to "steep" roadway access gate fees charged by the nonprofit North Maine Woods (see the Forestland Conservation Chapter for more detail), and the Raymonds decided against renting the summertime cabins they had built. They then catered to snowmobilers who paid no North Maine Woods gate fees for vehicles because they used trails instead, and sold gas, food, and supplies at their store. The snowmobile trails groomed by Raymond's were sometimes used by 2,000 snowmobiles on weekends.

In the summer and fall, there are many roads to explore in a vehicle or ATV, and a public boat launch is located nearby at Norcross Brook.

Fall brings the different time frames of hunting season, offering a variety of abundant wildlife for the hunter or the pleasure of viewing unexpected wildlife in its natural habitat. After open water fishing

Northeast Carry – Winnegarnock House and Supply Store – Raymond's Country Store

from May to October, the arrival of winter months creates an ice fishing mecca with miles of snowmobiling and fishing opportunities. The location is completely self-sufficient with an off-grid lifestyle and business.

After a run of 43 years, in 2021 the Raymonds decided to sell their Raymond's Country Store and seven-acre property at Northeast Carry which offers gasoline, firewood, propane gas, storage units, a store, home cooked food, cabins to rent, and a place to call home year-round.

Northeast Carry – Winnegarnock House and Supply Store – Raymond's Country Store

Northeast Carry in 2008. Internet photos from a real estate sales website.

Northwest Carry - Seboomook House - Seboomook Campground

Northwest Carry gets its name from the 1½-mile overland route it provides from Carry Brook at the head of Moosehead's Northwest Bay to reach the West Branch of the Penobscot River near the present day Seboomook dam. The route was an historic one, taken by indigenous peoples traveling from the lower reaches of the Penobscot River, across Moosehead Lake, to Quebec. At Northwest Carry, the route went up Carry Brook, reaching the portage path to Meadow Pond and on to the West Branch.

The first permanent building constructed at Seboomook/Northwest Carry was a log structure which Marshall "Marsh" Lane, a logger and guide, built about 1840. Charles A.J. Farrar notes in his 1884 *Moosehead Lake, North Woods Wilderness*, that Lane's son Charles Ferdinand "Ferd" Lane "has erected a comfortable camp here, where good entertainment is offered to sportsmen, and also keeps a team to haul canoes and supplies across the carry, which is a mile and a half long." The Lanes established a farm and supporting services for travelers, loggers, adventurers, and sports who wanted to reach the West Branch or needed a place to rest before continuing the .4 miles up Carry Brook. As paddlers went up the brook, Lane hitched up his team and took the Canada Road to the portage with canoes and gear to meet them.

Ferd left his father's shanty standing for use, but built a new, more comfortable structure for travelers at Seboomook.

The Lanes must have enjoyed a reasonably strong guiding business given that Alec (Alexander) Lessard, a Greenville guide and farmer, either bought the business or managed it in Ferdinand's absence.

Joseph Morris (b.1823) and his family moved from their well-known Morris Farm on the West Branch at the carry to Northwest Bay to

Northwest Carry – Seboomook House – Seboomook Campground

take over the operation from Alec in 1886. Morris built the first formal-looking hotel that year and called it "Seboomook House." Morris had experienced the shortcomings of the shallow water at Northeast Carry for steamboats carrying both loggers and sports, and their equipment, and sited the hotel, a small wharf, and a storage barn on the point at the head of Northwest Bay rather than in the Carry Brook inlet because the point had deeper water for wharf access.

Given some personal circumstances of the Morris family, it appears that Morris had Bill Young (b.1862), a guide and son of a Greenville printer, operate the hotel beginning about 1888. Young, who was single at the time, married his wife Annie in 1890.

Joseph Morris died in 1891, and probate court records confirmed that he owned the hotel at Northwest Carry. The 1895 settlement of his estate included the sale of the hotel, but the records did not list the purchaser. Historian Bill Geller presumes Milton G. Shaw, the well-established Bath lumberman and investor in the Coburn Steamship Company on Moosehead Lake, was probably the new owner.

By 1894, Martin P. and Nellie E. Colbath, farmers from Exeter, Maine, apparently leased the Morris establishment and opened the post office by 1895. Colbath bought the property from Shaw in 1899. At the time, the site had a small wharf and storehouse that Morris had built. By 1912, Colbath's wharf extensions lengthened it to 220' and the storehouse was 248' in length. Over time, Colbath added other buildings, including a general store that opened by 1904, an annex to the hotel, and a blacksmith shop. These new buildings were built on an additional 9 19/32nds acres (in the adjacent Big W township) purchased from Milton G. Shaw. In the deeds, Shaw retained rights for steamships to pass to and from the wharf and anything else supporting his lumbering operations until he ceased such interests.

SEBOOMOOK HOUSE,

SEBOOMOOK (Northwest Carry), **MOOSEHEAD LAKE, ME.**

Beautifully situated at head of lake, commanding unsurpassed view. One of best fishing and hunting resorts in Maine. Splendid trout fishing. Deer come in sight of house. Guides and canoes furnished. Canoes and outfits transported across the carry.

Interesting feature in neighborhood are great log sluice, carrying one million feet of logs from Penobscot to Kennebec waters every 24 hours; and Seboomook Falls (famed in verse and story), on the west branch of the Penobscot.

House recently enlarged and renovated. Every room pleasant. A high-class family resort. Daily mails in summer. **Rates, $2 a day. Special rates to families.** Letters promptly answered.

M. P. COLBATH, (P. O). SEBOOMOOK, ME.

In the Maine Woods ad, 1901.

Colbath died in 1919, and his wife, Nellie, feeling the strain from trying to run the entire operation, began to sell off the land and structures in 1921. She sold the "hotel property" east of the road from the wharf, excepting the plot with the store she owned per a 1918 deed, to Ralph L. Keating of Portland, Maine. By 1922, Keating was advertising the establishment as the Northwest Inn.

Also in 1922, Nellie and GNP Co. negotiated an agreement for a company crew to rebuild the storehouse, add a conveyor, and enlarge the wharf so it could handle any steamer on the lake.

Keating operated during the 1924 season, but in November 1924 he sold his "hotel property" and buildings to J. Otis Wardwell of Haverhill, Massachusetts, and bought the west parcel (in Big W Township) from Nellie.

Wardwell continued the inn operation and in 1928 he bought the Nellie Colbath store lot from GNP Co.

NORTHWEST INN

ON MOOSEHEAD LAKE

Trout fishing from May until October. 130 miles of wilderness macadam roads lead you to the most remote fishing places. Some of these new roads now put the fishermen on waters where few have ever wet a line.

Vacations spent here during July and August will long be remembered, as the scenic beauty of Northern Moosehead with its islands and surrounding mountains is spread out before the Inn. Outdoor games, excellent bathing, canoeing, etc.

Hunting of partridge and deer unsurpassed. Game easily handled for shipment.   *References and booklets on request.*

Ralph L. Keating, Proprietor, Seboomook, Maine

In the Maine Woods ad, 1923.

In 1928, Keating sold the west parcel including all buildings and the wharf, to GNP Co. Previously, GNP Co. only had access-to-the-lake rights and paid rent for the use of the wharf. GNP Co. owned the land abutting the north boundary line of the once Colbath properties, whereon was located its Seboomook farm.

Beginning about 1930, Keating hired Washington Irving Hamilton, and perhaps his wife Laura, as caretakers. Washington, who was born in 1872 at Kokadjo, guided out of Greenville from a young age. The Hamiltons were long-time residents of Greenville, and by 1920 they were hotel proprietors living on West Street in Greenville. They leased the Kokad-Jo Inn on First Roach Pond on the eastern side of the lake and spent 15 years as proprietors of the inn.

The couple purchased the Seboomook House in 1930 and moved to Northwest Bay. In August 1933, Laura bought the whole of the Otis Wardwell properties. The Hamiltons enlarged the hotel and did a good business up until WWII began to restrict travel.

They did not open the hotel in 1944 and it burned to the ground on April 9, 1945, ignited by a grass fire that wasn't completely extinguished. About 100 men fought the blaze but could not control it. W. Irving Hamilton was the sole occupant of the hotel at the time. Given that business was dying out, the Hamiltons decided not to rebuild, and GNP Co. purchased the property in 1922.[40]

The Bradstreet Project. In response to requests from timberland owners, in 1893 the state legislature gave its approval to send logs harvested from the upper reaches of the Penobscot drainage basin into Moosehead Lake. Prior to that time, all harvested timber had been sent down the West Branch of the Penobscot.

The result was "The Bradstreet Project," which consisted of two 600' conveyors, a dam on Carry Brook to impound water to release into a sluiceway, and the sluiceway itself to Moosehead Lake. Logs for sawmills on the Kennebec River were brought from Seboomook Lake on the West Branch on the two conveyors or "endless chains" to Carry Pond, from which point they were floated by the water released into the sluiceway from Carry Pond into Moosehead Lake at Northwest Carry. The Bradstreet Project operated for eight years, and 8-10 million board feet of pine, spruce, and cedar were moved via the conveyor and sluice system each year.[41]

Once in Moosehead Lake, logs were gathered into booms towed down the lake by steam-powered logging towboats, as shown in the following photograph, and sluiced through the east outlet dam into the Kennebec River to the sawmills.[42]

At varying times, the steamboats *Twilight,* or *Gov. Coburn,* or *Katahdin* towed log booms of 20-30 acres in size to the east outlet for sluicing down the Kennebec.

Northwest Carry – Seboomook House – Seboomook Campground

Log boom "bag" being towed past Mt. Kineo to the east outlet.
The Northern magazine cover photo, June 1927, by The Baker Studio.

The Bradstreet Project operation ran for only eight years, because the Seboomook Dam Company property and rights to the conveyor/sluiceway were bought by GNP Co. The purchase ensured that all the harvested timber in the entire West Branch watershed by the GNP Co. was floated down the West Branch to its massive paper mill in Millinocket, rather than into the Kennebec River via Moosehead Lake.

GNP Co. replaced the Bradstreet-built 1912 Seboomook dam on the West Branch in 1936 with a concrete dam having 28' of head; the dam expanded the Seboomook Lake impoundment up to Pittston Farm, (at the confluence of the North and South Branches of the Penobscot River) a distance of 13 miles. The dam, combined with other West Branch dams, secured the West Branch as the water-based route for pulpwood being sent to Millinocket.

Northwest Carry – Seboomook House – Seboomook Campground

Seboomook and St. John Railroad. Between 1914 and 1921, GNP Co. planned and began construction on an 18-mile standard gauge railroad line to haul pulpwood from the St. John River watershed to Seboomook Lake on the West Branch, from which point it was to be sent down the West Branch to the Millinocket paper mills owned by GNP Co. The project was estimated to be a less expensive option than the alternative of improving the north-flowing St. John River for log driving.

The 10'-13' depth water at Northwest Carry meant construction of a relatively short wharf was far more feasible than the Northeast Carry location for the off-loading of logging equipment to clear the right-of-way and deliver the locomotive and the rail cars needed to help build the rail line. In 1920, GNP Co. expanded the Seboomook wharf and storehouse and developed a large farm nearby to construct more boarding space for its work crews, to provide stables for the draft horses involved in right-of-way clearing, and to establish gardens for lumber camp food and hayfields for animal feed.

Locomotive (Climax No. 2) and rolling stock of 15–20 cars (each capable of holding about 10 cords) came up Moosehead Lake on barges to the Seboomook wharf. Once offloaded, the locomotive steamed over the partially built line to Pittston Farm and was rolled onto a scow built at the farm and moved across Seboomook Lake to the South Terminal (this terminal was on the north shore of Seboomook Lake). The engine rolled on the first seven miles of track by September 1921 when it began making a daily trip to No. 5 Camp where a crew put up another sawmill in support of the rail line project. By June 1922, the "burning crew" had cleared the line to within 1.5 miles of its end point. At the South Terminal in 1921 was a crew of about 700. The track use strategy called for two standard gauge locomotives. Only one was delivered, however, because the other only got as far as Greenville when GNP Co. sold it back to the company from which it was purchased.[43]

Despite the tremendous expense of clearing and building the railroad 50' right-of-way, leveling the bed, and placing ties and the rails, no wood was ever hauled for the mills. In October 1928 new GNP Co.

President William Whitcomb permanently suspended the project. Construction crews had set down only 12.5 miles of track and the only wood hauled on this rail line was 1,000 cords cut on the right of way. The following summer a crew removed the railroad equipment and took up the rails between Northwest Bay and Pittston Farm. Whitcomb apparently decided that the expenses of the rail operation exceeded alternatives for getting the logs cut in the same area into the North Branch of the Penobscot.[44]

Prisoner of War Camp. In 1944, the GNP Co. Seboomook farm was converted to a German prisoner of war compound, and the hotel did not open because the United States was fully engaged in WWII. H&W was the only company in the U.S. making "tabulating card stock" paper which was in great demand by the U.S. armed forces. The prisoners harvested softwood pulp from which the paper was made, and each prisoner was responsible for cutting one cord per day using axes and crosscut saws. It was reported that the prisoners cut 34,000 cords of pulp from 1944-46. Between 200 and 250 prisoners were housed and fed using facilities at GNP Co.'s Seboomook farm.[45]

In 1948, GNP Co. demolished its buildings on the site, and the Seboomook Wilderness Campground was established there.

Seboomook Campground. Today, the Seboomook Wilderness Campground offers waterfront campsites with water and electric hookups, and several lean-to shelters. A modern bathhouse provides hot showers and flush toilets. About eight cabins are available, ranging from a primitive shelter to beautiful modern housekeeping cabins with fully equipped kitchens and full baths. There is a children's playground and a small marina with boat slips available. Boat rentals include canoes, kayaks, and a 14' boat with an outboard.

Northwest Carry – Seboomook House – Seboomook Campground

Seboomook Wilderness Campground. campspot.com

maineanencyclopedia.com

The general store is stocked with groceries, beer, camping supplies, gift items, and ice; propane, gasoline, and firewood are available.

Randall's Camps - Chadwick's Camps - West Branch Pond Camps

West Branch Pond Camps is the oldest continually operating family-owned sporting camp in Maine.

Originally known as Randall's Camps, Philip H. Randall and his son Charles established them in 1880 on land leased from Hollingsworth and Whitney (H&W) on First West Branch Pond. The site was that of an old logging camp with an existing long-log building. By 1889, Randall had added two additional hunting cabins and was working on a third.

P. H. Randall's West Branch Pond Camps, *Maine and Its Scenic Wonders*, Geo. W. Morris, Portland, Maine, 1898.

Randall's Camps – Chadwick's Camps – West Branch Pond Camps

Charles Randall was a "pioneer" in the sporting camp business and gradually the number of buildings grew to about 20 that could accommodate 30-35 "sports." Early guests arrived by train in Greenville and took a steamer to Lily Bay. They then traveled by buckboard about seven miles to Kokadjo at First Roach Pond and then five more miles to reach West Branch Pond.

Charles Randall sold the camp buildings in 1914 to Lewis Chadwick, who operated them until 1921 before selling them to his brother Fred. Fred and his wife Abbie Savage owned and managed the camps until 1949.

In 1950, the Chadwicks sold the camps to Constance and Clifton Kealiher, who were the Chadwicks' daughter and son-in-law.

Collection of the Moosehead Historical Society (detail), #2008.70.000.

Randall's Camps – Chadwick's Camps – West Branch Pond Camps

> **CHADWICK'S CAMPS** West Branch Ponds
>
> Trout are plentiful in the different ponds and fine brook fishing. Moose, deer, birds and other small game in abundance. Cream, Milk, Eggs and Vegetables from our farm. Terms $2.00 and $2.50 per day. For further information and our booklet address
>
> **L. P. CHADWICK**
> KOKAD-JO, MAINE

In the Maine Woods ad, 1914.

In 1960, the Kealihers purchased from the Guy Gannett Publishing Co., Inc. the original "Howell's" camp on the site. It had been remodeled and reconditioned and was known as the "Gannett Camp." The Guy Gannett Publishing owned the *Portland Press Herald*, the *Waterville Morning Sentinel,* and other newspapers, and the WGAN radio and television stations in Portland.

Remarkably, when the camps were sold again in 1975, the new owners were from the third generation of Chadwicks, daughter Carol and husband Andrew Stirling.[46]

West Branch Pond Camps remain a wilderness refuge in Maine's north woods. Guests can stay in the same historic log cabins that adventurous outdoorsmen did a century before, but with all the modern conveniences that make them feel at home. This natural Maine paradise near prominent White Cap Mountain provides hearty home-cooked meals to keep guests comfortable and well-nourished. There is a camp library, and board games are available in the "casino." Each cabin has wood heat from an open fireplace; electric lights are powered by a generator. The 10:00 pm "lights out" tradition lets guests truly relax. Modern living meets rustic beauty and north woods tradition at West Branch Pond Camps. Trout are the primary fishing resource on the First, Second, and Third West Branch Ponds, although there are some salmon. Fishing is limited to fly-fishing-only, but those who are not fishing can enjoy the

Randall's Camps – Chadwick's Camps – West Branch Pond Camps

swimming, canoeing, or hiking on trails including those to the top of White Cap Mountain. The Appalachian Mountain Club's Gorman Chairback Lodge & Camps and the AMC Medawisla Lodge and Camps are nearby.

The Appalachian Mountain Club's Gorman Chairback Lodge & Camps, and the AMC Medawisla Lodge and Camps, are nearby.

Collection of The Moosehead Historical Society (detail), # 99.6.10.

Randall's Camps – Chadwick's Camps – West Branch Pond Camps

1881 Dining Room. westbranchpondcamps.com

Second Roach Pond Camps – Medawisla

Second Roach Pond Camps. The Roach River runs into Moosehead Lake's Spencer Bay on its eastern shore. First Roach Pond is seven miles up the river and in the 1890s the Roach River House was established at the pond's outlet.

The Second Roach Pond Camps were located on Second Roach Pond which is about 1½ miles above the head of First Roach. The river is famous for its square-tailed trout and salmon fisheries. Because its waters are a breeding ground for trout, the Roach River system is closed to ice fishing. In the 1920s, a logging camp run by Mr. and Mrs. W.A. Chase, was built at Second Roach Pond near the dam to support logging operations of Hollingsworth and Whitney (H&W).

Roy O'Donnell had started out as a guide in the 1930s and was well-known on the Roach River system of ponds. He also had become a bush pilot with his own flying service, taking fly fishermen into remote ponds. In the 1940s, he began O'Donnell's Flying service in Greenville. The Second Roach logging campsite was leased by Roy and his wife Louise, and they built seven cabins for hunting and fishing clientele to add to the existing main lodge.

After Roy died in the mid-1960s, Louise married Fred Rogers. They ran the camps until 1982 when they sold them to guide Bill Holland and his wife Nancy. The Hollands made needed improvements, such as jacking up the cabins and replacing any rotted sills. Porches were added, new stoves were purchased, and a stone fireplace was built in the lodge. In 1983, Raymond and Elizabeth Kulp became proprietors for the Hollands, and the Hollands sold the site and buildings to Edward "Russ" and Mimi Pratt Whitten in 1986. Before they bought the Second Roach Pond Camps, the Whittens had gained experience by operating seasonal sporting camps on nearby Lobster Lake. They

Second Roach Pond Camps – Medawisla

renamed the sporting camp "Medawisla," which means "loon" in the Wabanaki language.

Shannon and Larry LeRoy bought the Medawisla camps from the Whittens in 1992 and operated them for 14 years before selling them to the Appalachian Mountain Club (AMC) in 2006.

Medawisla. For several years, AMC ran operations out of the existing camps; but in 2012, they closed their doors for a major renovation. AMC did an assessment for determining the future design of the lodge and camp facility, and it was verified that the old lodge and camp buildings were in somewhat poor condition. It was decided a better long-term option was to tear everything down and rebuild. AMC looked at how to fit the new facility into the landscape, and the new main lodge was set back from the shoreline and placed on higher ground, so it had less impact on the lakeside environment. Two other eco-friendly aspects of the facility are its modern composting toilets and the main lodge's roof which is covered with 60 solar panels producing more than 19 kilowatts of energy. AMC predicted the panels would provide at least 60 percent of the lodge's energy consumption, with the rest being produced by a generator.

Medawisla lodge interior photo. outdoors.org

Second Roach Pond Camps – Medawisla

The new Medawisla opened in 2017 and looks very much like the two other nearby AMC camps, Gorman Chairback Lodge & Cabins, and Little Lyford Lodge & Cabins. One difference, though, is that at those two AMC camps, some of the old cabins were able to be saved.

Medawisla lodge exterior photo. outdoors.org.

Medawisla provides an ideal spot for exploring the famed 100-Mile Wilderness portion of The Appalachian Trail.

Altogether, the campus includes a boat launch and waterfront pavilion, two bunkhouses, a bathhouse, and nine private cabins. The central lodge features a spacious dining room, lounge, kitchens, bathrooms, and sauna.

Recreational opportunities include hiking, paddling, fly-fishing, canoe-camping, snowshoeing, and cross-country skiing, just steps away from private cabin or bunkhouse accommodations.

Second Roach Pond Camps – Medawisla

Winter guests have access to more than 30 miles of groomed cross-country ski trails around the lodge, plus an additional 80 miles of lodge-to-lodge groomed trails. Located a day apart by ski or snowshoe, guests can travel from Medawisla to the historic West Branch Pond Camps, and to AMC's Little Lyford Camps, and finally AMC's Gorman Chairback Camps. Complementary snowshoes are available. A shuttle transports hiking gear to the next lodge, providing the freedom to ski or snowshoe with just a day pack. Shuttle service is also available so that a vehicle can be waiting at the end of a trip.

Summer guests can enjoy a waterfront campfire or paddle Second Roach Pond using complementary kayaks, canoes, and paddle boards. The roofed pavilion offers a place for gathering, and a propane grill is available for those taking the self-service food option.

Meals are included in full-service nightly rates, but guests taking the self-service option may purchase individual meals at the lodge. Breakfast is served family-style, made-to-order trail lunches are available at breakfast, and dinner is also served family-style.

Cabins/bunkhouses include a two-burner stove, utensils, and service ware. All share a central bathhouse with composting toilets and hot showers.

American Disability Act (ADA) accessibility is provided in two cabins. The main lodge, dining hall, central bathhouse, and meeting space are ADA accessible, and hardened gravel paths run throughout.

Spencer Bay Camps - Casey's Campground

Spencer Bay is known as one of the best fishing areas on Moosehead Lake, but it's also a favorite of many families for the natural, unspoiled beauty of the surrounding mountains, spectacular sunrises and sunsets, and the lake itself. From deeds recorded in the Piscataquis County Registry of Deeds, the Spencer Bay camps site was leased by camp operators from a succession of timberland owners: first M.G. Shaw, then Hollingsworth and Whitney, and lastly Scott Paper Company.

Stevens Point, at the mouth of Spencer Bay at the "Narrows," was occupied in 1901 by the new Stuart and Stevens sporting camps.

THESE NEW SPORTING CAMPS are located at Spencer Narrows, on Moosehead Lake, Maine, in one of the finest localities for big game hunting to be found in any part of the state. Lve. Boston 7 p.m., arr. Bangor 3.30 a.m.; lve. Bangor 7 a.m., via B. & A. R.R., arr. Greenville 10.50 a.m., connecting with steamer for Lily Bay, where parties will be met with launch, arriving at camps about 2 o'clock p.m.

SPORTSMEN wishing an outing and desirous of securing their number of big game will make no mistake in coming to our camps. In season, **Ice Fishing** is excellent and those who drive up will find shelter and feed for their horses.

TERMS, $2 per day; $10 per week. GUIDES furnished on short notice.

STUART & STEVENS, Proprietors.

Post Office, LILY BAY, MAINE.

In the Maine Woods ad, 1905.

The 15-acre Stevens Point property, in Township A, Range 14, WELS, was leased from H&W and encompassed a half-mile of water frontage with a protected marina.

Spencer Bay Camps – Casey's Campground

Ervin G. Stevens marketed the camps as the Spencer Narrows Camps in the 1920s.

In the Maine Woods ad, 1926.

Spencer Narrows Camps postcard. Collection of The Moosehead Historical Society (detail), #2009.07.39.

Amory and Elizabeth Houghton purchased the Spencer Bay Camps from Ervin Stevens in 1935 and owned them through the 1950s. All cabins had electric lights, baths, open Franklin stoves, and excellent beds. Meals were supplied in the main lodge.

> **HOUGHTON'S**
> **SPENCER BAY CAMPS**
> **MOOSEHEAD LAKE, MAINE**
>
> A small resort on the shore of Moosehead Lake, for the fisherman and his family. Excellent food, all modern comforts. Congenial clientele.
>
> **Tariff: $7.00 daily**   Special rates for children
>
> Guests met with camp cruiser by appointment, no charge.
> Above all! Peace—Rest—Quiet
> **Write now for particulars**
> AMORY and ELIZABETH HOUGHTON
>
> **SPENCER BAY CAMPS   GREENVILLE, MAINE**
> Established 1900
> Limited Accommodations   Telephone Greenville 6 ring 4

Maine Invites You ad, 1945. Maine Publicity Bureau, digital commons at the Bangor Public Library.

Caretakers for the camps during 1937-39 were Moosehead area guide Eddie McKeen and his wife and Verna. They stayed through the winters by themselves to take care of the cow and chickens, and handled other odd jobs as needed. During the rest of the year, Verna did all the cooking and laundry for the sports.

The Spencer Bay Club, a private hunting and fishing club, was also located on the Stevens Point property (see the Private Sporting Clubs chapter).

Spencer Bay Camps – Casey's Campground

> **Eastman's Spencer Bay Camps**
> ON MOOSEHEAD LAKE
>
> For a relaxing family vacation. "Off the beaten trail"
> Individual cabins with full bath. American Plan
> Write for detailed information and illustrated folder.
> Owned and operated by TOM and MARG EASTMAN
> Address: Greenville, Maine   Phone OXbow 5-2801

Maine Invites You ad, 25th edition, 1959. Maine Publicity Bureau, digital commons at the Bangor Public Library.

L. Thornton ("Tom") Eastman and Marjorie ("Marg") Eastman sold the Stevens Point buildings and equipment to Harold and Esther Pattershall in 1963, and they remained the owners and operators of the camps until about 1980.

In 1992, Verdell ("Casey") L. LaCasce purchased the 15.25-acre Stevens Point site from Skylark, Inc., Scott Paper Company's land sales and leasing entity. Casey's Spencer Bay Campground's ten waterfront "housekeeping" log cabins on Stevens Point could accommodate from four to twelve people, but guests needed to bring their own bedding and towels. Generators supplied power for a few hours in the morning and again in the afternoon. Cabins were open from May 15th through the end of November when the deer and moose hunting seasons ended.

The campground could accommodate some RV's, some with electrical power hookups. There was a large shower house for campers, with private hot showers, sinks, and flush toilets. Casey's permanently closed in 2020 and was listed for sale.

Spencer Pond Camps

Deep in the woods (14 miles from the nearest neighbors and the only cabins on Spencer Pond) the six rustic-cozy Spencer Pond cabins and their surroundings offer a piece of living history amidst scenic beauty. Guests enjoy the beauty and bounty of pristine natural surroundings, fish, hike, hunt, canoe, read, nap, bird watch, mountain bike, photograph, stargaze, and build campfires.

In 1901, Mose Duty, a young Maine guide and boat builder, started clearing land for what would become Spencer Pond Camps. Duty was a native of the area, having been born on a 200-acre Moosehead Lake farm near Spencer Bay. In 1908, Duty married Lillian Lamarr, who lived on the 200-acre parcel next door. One of the men he guided, a Mr. Stetson, was a key official of the Oxford Paper Company in Rumford, Maine, which owned the entire Days Academy Township around the pond.

Duty told Stetson that he had always wanted a camp on Spencer Pond. Stetson told him to pick out the spot he wanted, and then leased the land to him. At age 21, Duty built a big cabin there and named it "Sabotowan," the Abenaki name for nearby Big Spencer Mountain.

Stetson was also a member of the William Tell Club (see the Private Sporting Clubs chapter) whose members were wealthy businessmen. The club's lodge had been built on a high banking overlooking Spencer Pond's outlet stream, on nearby Hollingsworth and Whitney (H&W) land. In 1950, George Dulac heard that the William Tell Club was closing. Dulac asked Stetson if he could take down the buildings and bring the materials over to the northwest shore of Spencer Pond so he could build some small camps there, and after a period of uncertainty Oxford Paper finally agreed.

Duty died in 1944, and Lillian sold the camp to George and Louise Dulac and Mr. and Mrs. Fred Thompson. The two wives were sisters born on the Ronco Farm next to Duty. After two years, the Dulacs bought-out the Thompsons and made plans to operate a sporting camp. The land was still leased from Oxford Paper Company, though, and Oxford at first refused to give permission to operate a sporting camp there. Issues were resolved, and in 1948 Spencer Pond Cabins was established as a sporting camp for the first time. The Dulacs owned and operated the camps for 25 years, but George developed arthritis in his back. They decided to sell, and the Oxford Paper Company, having adjusted to the site being used for a sporting camp, insisted that it be sold as one parcel with the six cabins included.

Scott Paper Company, which had acquired H&W in 1954, owned vast amounts of forest land on the east side of Moosehead, including the land at the pond's outlet, and planned a large lumber operation where the club had been located.

In 1969, Anne Howe heard the Spencer Pond sporting camp was for sale and in the fall drove to the outlet of the pond following the road built by Scott Paper Company; she and her husband Charles "Chick" Howe purchased the camp. The Howes operated the cabins for 25 years and built two additional cabins. They decided to retire for health reasons in 1994.

SPENCER POND CAMPS
A family vacation that's different

The luxury of being alone! Private Driveway. No telephone or plumbing. Nature trails, Mountain climbing, fishing. Remote log cabins in the heart of Maine. Housekeeping only.
Brochure
Chick and Anne Howe   RFD; Greenville, Me. 04441

Maine Invites You ad, 1980. Maine Publicity Bureau.

The Howes financed the sale to Jill Martel and Bob Croce who operated the business for 14 years, until about 2008. Bob and Jill focused on ecotourism, fly fishing, and shoreland protection and monitoring; they also actively engaged guests in gardening projects, cabin repairs from sills to masonry, building a new back porch on the home camp, and expanding the trail system.

They also continued the long-established traditions of vegetable and flower gardens and enclosures for chickens. Although the camps were accessible by road, guests dropped off their supplies at their camp, then moved their cars to a parking area by the entry gate.

Spencer Pond Camps lodge. spencerpond.com

Beginning in 2010, Spencer Pond Camps were hosted for the next decade by Anne and Chick's granddaughter Christine Howe and her husband Dana Black (both registered Maine Guides), who provided guests with a true nostalgic wilderness experience as it was off-the-grid, which allowed its guests to experience what life was like at camps in the late 19th century. During this period, along with the support of the property owners, Dana executed a tremendous restoration to all the cabins and most of the outbuildings, replacing all sills and rotten logs, rebuilding every porch and several outhouses, adding log siding, and new pine interior walls and floors, and new steel roofs.

Spencer Pond Camps

Glen and Sarah Horne leased the camps in 2020. Glen now leases the camps himself, under Coyote Ridge Guide Service and Outfitting LLC, and operates them with his girlfriend Holly Todd.

The cabins have no electricity, but each has a fully equipped kitchen with a propane refrigerator and gas stove (cooktop and oven) with all cooking utensils, pots and pans, dishes, etc. Many "old-fashioned" kitchen tools allow guests to mix cakes, perk coffee (or use a French press), and make toast. Hand water pumps are inside each kitchen at the sink and provide water for washing and cleaning.

Cabins have kerosene and gas lights, and each cabin has its own private, clean outhouse. Shower stalls are inside each cabin, and hot showers can be taken by heating water on the wood stove and filling the solar shower bags or filling them and allowing them to heat in the sun.

There is a central fireplace where guests are welcome to build a bonfire and toast marshmallows, make s'mores, tell ghost stories, or simply enjoy the flicker of a moonlit fire.

The website for Spencer Pond Camps invites guests to "**S**tep back in time into six 'off the grid' authentic wilderness lakeside housekeeping cabins – each with its own unique personality. The cabins have no electricity but are fully furnished for comfort - with homemade quilts, games, cozy spots to relax, and warm woodstoves. Cabins have docks, and canoes, kayaks, and mountain bikes are included at no extra charge so guests can enjoy fishing, watching wildlife, and paddling on Spencer Pond. Screened porches on each camp allow sitting comfortably, listening to yodeling loons, or enjoying the quiet whispering of the wind through the pines. No need to pack a tent, sleeping bag, tarps, cookstove, or camper trailer, these cabins have everything you will need." [47]

A cabin interior, Spencer Pond Camps. Facebook.

Squaw Mountain Inn - Moose Mountain Inn

About a mile north of the Bangor & Aroostook Railroad terminal at Greenville Junction near Squaw Mountain (now renamed Big Moose Mountain) the new, modern, Squaw Mountain Inn opened in 1915 under the ownership of Arthur Crafts.

In the Maine Woods ad, 1923.

Squaw Mountain Inn – Moose Mountain Inn

Its attractions were "superior," and with a location that was especially advantageous for fishing, its first season highly successful.

(Readers will note in the Northeast Carry chapter, that from 1904-1926 Arthur Crafts also served as president of the Penobscot Hotel and Trading Company at Northeast Carry.)

Prior to being converted to an inn and camps, from 1901-1909 the buildings on the site comprised the Moosehead Lake Sanatorium. An ad for the sanatorium in the 1907 *Piscataquis Directory* proclaimed:

> Moosehead Lake Sanatorium, GREENVILLE JUNCTION, ME.
> SITUATED AT THE FOOT OF SQUAW MOUNTAIN,
> Commanding one of the prettiest views of the Lake.
> No Contagious diseases Received. Has the finest Surgical Record of any Hospital in the United States. Convalescents and those suffering from Nervous Troubles especially catered to. Accommodations furnished in the Main Building, Camps or Tents.
> Write for Booklet. L. F. HATCH, President.

Maine Invites You, 1949. Maine Publicity Bureau.

Philip Sheridan and Julia Crafts Sheridan owned and managed the Squaw Mountain Inn starting about 1924, and in 1964 leased it to Donald Lewis. The lease agreement gave Lewis the right to purchase the land and buildings within 60 days, an option which he exercised in early 1965.

In early 1971, Donald Lewis and son Donald Lewis, Jr. sold to the Squaw Mountain Development Corporation. Later in 1971, the Ski & Shore Development Associates purchased the real estate and buildings from the Squaw Mountain Development Corporation, and in 1972 sold it to Smile Inc, the general partner of the Condominium Resort Trust, a Limited Partnership. From 1974-1976 the property was subdivided and approximately 43 individual lots were developed and sold.

Here's the Outing Chance You've Longed for — at

Squaw Mountain Inn
MOOSEHEAD LAKE

One mile from Bangor & Aroostook and Canadian Pacific R. R. Stations

BIG FISH	IDEAL LIFE
Trout, Togue, Salmon, etc. right in front of the house and close by.	Care-free, healthful days in a wonderful scenic section of woods and water.

You'll find comfort and all-round enjoyment at SQUAW MOUNTAIN INN; also light, airy rooms with private baths, modern furnishings, steam heat. Our table is supplied with the best foods, vegetables, eggs, milk and cream, fresh from our own farm; absolutely pure spring water. Long distance telephone and telegraph service. Two daily mails.

Camps having bathroom, hot and cold water for two, three or four people, also a large log camp of eight rooms for large parties or families.

Meals are served in main dining room. Music, afternoon tea, during July and August.

A nine-hole golf course on the Inn grounds. Tennis court. Motor boats, row boats and canoes for hire. Good automobile road right to our door. Commodious garage.

OPEN MAY 8 FOR SEASON OF 1926

Write for Picture Booklet and Detailed Information

ARTHUR A. CRAFTS, Prop.   PHIL SHERIDAN, Manager

Greenville Junction, Maine

In the Maine Woods, ad, 1926.

Squaw Mountain Inn – Moose Mountain Inn

Julia Crafts Sheridan was born February 5, 1891, the only daughter of Arthur A. and Rebecca W. (Eveleth) Crafts. She was a life-long resident of Greenville and died in 1970.

She was actively connected with her father-in-law John Henry Eveleth in his extensive business enterprises. She is most remembered, though, for overseeing management of the Squaw Mountain Inn, which her father purchased when it was the shuttered Moosehead Sanatorium. Julia bought the inn from her mother and the sanatorium was completely remodeled. It re-opened as the inn about 1915 under the proprietorship of Arthur Crafts.

Julia was married to Rennie Philip Sheridan of Syracuse, New York, in a big gala ceremony at Syracuse in 1923. The following year, after having visited the Princess Hotel in Bermuda to learn the hotel business, Julia and Philip began managing the inn and Julia successfully operated it until 1964 when it was sold to a group of investors.

Julia E. Crafts Sheridan and R. Philip Sheridan also owned the 980-acre Farm Island near Mt. Kineo which they gifted to the state of Maine in 1971.

Philip and Julia Crafts Sheridan bequeathed the early 1890s Eveleth-Crafts-Sheridan House on Pritham Avenue in Greenville to the Moosehead Historical Society to commemorate the economic, social, and cultural heritage of the region. The mansion, the carriage house, barn, and grounds were once part of the old Moosehead Inn property owned by the Crafts. The spectacular landscaping, particularly the sunken garden, became a showcase for residential horticulture in the early 20th century.

"The Long Legacy of Julia Crafts Sheridan – Moosehead Historical Society" mooseheadhistory.org, 2017.

Tomhegan Camps

In the early 1900s, Russell Parker Spinney graduated from Bryant and Stratton Business College in Concord, New Hampshire, but did not like city living. He made his way to the Rangeley area and worked as a guide at Capt. Barker's camps. It was there he met his future bride Lilla Blanche, and they married in February 1910. Spinney brought her the six miles over the ice from Rockwood to Tomhegan by horse-drawn sled. On the sled were also a barrel of molasses, two barrels of flour, one barrel of salt pork, and other basic necessities.

The camps were built by the Spinneys and by Douglas Rollins, the Governor of New Hampshire, who bought 3,000 acres of land where the Tomhegan camps were to be built. There was no electricity, and during the winter, water had to be drawn from the lake by sawing a hole in the ice with a chainsaw. The only access to Tomhegan in

Tomhegan Camps Lodge. Collection of The Moosehead Historical Society (detail), #1997.18.51.

those days was by water from Rockwood, where clients came to Kineo Station by train and were picked up by one of the steamers on the lake and transported to Tomhegan. After reaching camp, the guests were catered to by the camp staff; meals were served three times a day and after the evening meal the guests were provided with a lantern to light their way back to their individual camps. Their fireplace fires were started by cabin boys and fresh spring water was brought in.

Tomhegan Camps lodge. tomhegancamps.com

The Rollins family eventually sold the camp and 127 acres to Spinney and kept the remaining acreage. After Russell Spinney's death in 1939, the camps were operated by his wife, Lilla, and their daughter Marjorie. Marjorie was born April 13, 1916, in cabin #4 "Diana." She married Keith McBurnie in 1950, and they had their honeymoon in cabin #1 "Hemlock." In 1951, Lilla passed away, leaving Marjorie and her husband Keith to maintain and keep Tomhegan going.

In 1954, Marjorie had an access road constructed from the Rockwood Road, creating a major accessibility change for Tomhegan. Keith and Marjorie managed the camps until 1977 when, due to a cancer diagnosis, Margaret sold the camps.[48]

Tomhegan Camps

However, Marjorie continued to live at Tomhegan in the "Winter Camp" until 2005, when she was no longer able to live alone and moved to Skowhegan. She passed away in October of 2007, at the age of 89. Her camp was rebuilt in the fall of 2007 and named "Margie" in her honor.

Marjorie was well known in the area for her love of wild animals, and most of the camps are named after pet deer she raised there. The deer were often seen feeding near her camp, and she had pictures of them inside the camp lying on her bed and under her Christmas tree. The doe "Diana" whose gravestone is situated near the pump house (in front of cabin #3), and "Ramona" were particular favorites. Diana raised 35 deer offspring during her 18½ years at Tomhegan.

Tomhegan's powerboat *Rosemary Girl* with guide Laurel Polyott and "sports" ready for fishing (detail). Collection of The Moosehead Historical Society #1997.18.43.

"Ferguson Point" at the camps was named after one of the early guests of Tomhegan. The story goes that Mrs. Ferguson fell in love with her Indian guide, and being a lady of means, she had several tents erected on the spot with red carpeting running between them. It was at Tomhegan Camps that they whiled away the summer days in romantic bliss.

Tomhegan Camps

A notable visitor was Gene Tunney, the one-time heavyweight boxing champion, who had trained at Miller's Training Camp at Harford's Point. He spent Christmas with Marjorie Spinney's family when she was only a small school-age child.

Another prominent visitor was Mrs. Alice Statler of the Hilton-Statler hotel chain, who spent the summers there from 1939 until just before her death in 1969. She made a significant financial contribution to rebuilding the camp's traditional boardwalk which stretched ¼ of a mile along the shoreline, connecting all the cabins and the lodge. It was rebuilt at her expense to make the walk easier as she got older.

Tomhegan boardwalk (detail). Collection of The Moosehead Historical Society #1997.18.53.

Between 1977 and 1983, the camps did not accommodate paying guests, although the squirrels, chipmunks, bats, and an assortment of other wildlife were in residence. In January 1983, Steve and Pam Rich purchased the camps, and they immediately began to rebuild the badly deteriorated individual cabins. Steve, skilled as both a carpenter and manager, first gutted out the "Guides Camp" and completely rebuilt it, making it their home. Then the cabins, one by one, were set back on their posts. All the plumbing was repaired or replaced, generator electrical wire replaced, new kitchens installed, porches or walls built, and, finally in September of 1984, electricity was brought in by a one-mile underwater cable from Rockwood to replace the generators. Pam was very particular about cleaning the camps and did most of it herself, along with painting, taking reservations, greeting guests, bookkeeping, and feeding the crews working on the camps.

In 1988, Tomhegan was purchased by a single owner, but once again became neglected. In 1993, the lodge and all the cabins except for #4, #5, and #6 were sold at auction.

Although camp owners had title to their individual cottages, the Tomhegan Camp Owners' Association was created to own the real estate. Camp owners are now required to be members of the Association, and Tomhegan remains unique on Moosehead Lake for this "collective" ownership.

To make the needed repairs to the cabins after 1993, every collective member/owner contributed toward the expense of the work. All the cabins were given new roofs, and it was made certain that each cabins had good wells and properly functioning or new septic systems. All the owners participate in the management costs for the collective's system of renting individual cabins and keeping the boardwalk maintained.

In 2008, the submarine cable was replaced by a utility pole line from the Pittston Farm Road to the camps.

Today, the nine cabins and lodge at Tomhegan Wilderness Cabins are all privately owned yet available for rent. Each is well-maintained and clean for the enjoyment of renters, along with 1½ miles of Moosehead Lake waterfront. The four-season home/lodge has eight rooms, including a large kitchen, and five bedrooms and baths.

Tomhegan Lodge. tomhegancamps.com

Managers of the Association from 2000 to 2016 were Leona and Norman Harding, and the current managers are Rick and Stacey Bridges.

Located in the middle of a 127-acre state game preserve with no hunting, Tomhegan treats guests to an abundance of peaceful wilderness and majestic wildlife and is open year-round.[49]

"Ramona," one of nine Tomhegan cabins. Tomhegancamps.com

Wheat's Island Camps

Two Mile Island (also known as Island #17) has been for many years a unique landmark that sits in the middle of Lily Bay. The island is one half-acre in size and located two miles by boat from several landing areas. It's 12 miles from the town of Greenville and sits on a famous "salmon shoal." In 1946, Alfred William Wheat, a former U.S. Navy Seabee, purchased the island and built a 1,494 sq. ft. rustic log lodge with a stone fireplace and 5 bedrooms. He called this location "Wheat's Island Camps" and offered hunting, fishing, and recreation. The island had several hundred feet of sandy beach shallow enough for children to enjoy safely.

Wheat wrote the following about his new sporting camp: "My camps are located in one of the best hunting and fishing spots in the United States for fishing, plenty of game fighting land locked [sic] salmon, togue (lake trout) and those grand old square tails (trout) that will make the heart of any angler skip a beat. Fly casting, trolling, and still fishing - it's all here. Hunting deer, bear, game, woodcock, grouse, ducks, and the kind of country you like to hunt … You will enjoy the lodge, good beds, main dining room and all home cooked food. A camp secluded and quiet, new boats, motors, and canoes."

Wheat paid-off his mortgage on the island property in 1954 but passed-away that same year. His widow Martha Wheat sold the island in 1976. It has been bought and sold by various private owners since. The island is once again known as Two Mile Island.

Wheat's Island. Real estate website photo

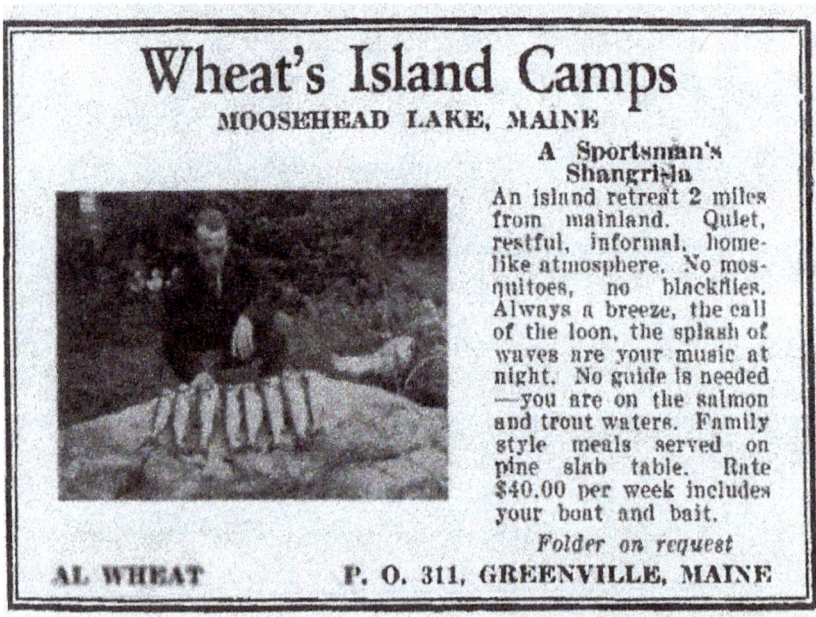
Maine Invites You ad, 1951. Maine Publicity Bureau.

Whitten's Store - Moosehead Inn and Cabins - Whitten's Cottages - Whitten's Lodge & Cabins

The Somerset Railroad constructed a line to Kineo Station at the settlement at Birch Point, now known as Rockwood, in 1906. The name Rockwood is believed to have come from Hiram Rockwood Page, who decided around 1909 that the railroad's Kineo Station needed a post office. Hence, he named the post office after himself.

Whitten's Store and Moosehead Inn. With the coming of the railroad to serve the expanding Mt. Kineo House Hotel and Resort, the population of Rockwood grew rapidly for a short time. A hotel was constructed there by a man named Champagne in the early 1900s. Guy Morton Whitten moved to Rockwood in 1908 with his wife Zelda (sometimes known as Eldie) and opened Whitten's Store in 1912, selling gifts and outfitting supplies. The original building was destroyed by fire in 1941 and was rebuilt in 1952. It was located on the "Rockwood Strip" on the old Route 15 at what is now the corner of Lake Street and Village Road.

Around the same time, a store owned by Ricker Hotel Company near Kineo Station was in operation, competing with Whitten's.

Whitten's Store – Moosehead Inn and Cabins – Whitten's Cottages – Whitten's Lodge & Cabins

MOOSEHEAD INN and CAMPS
ON MOOSEHEAD LAKE

New large cabins, overlooking the lake, with or without kitchenettes, also central dining room and cocktail lounge.

Salmon, Togue and Trout Fishing
Also Deer, Bear, and Partridge Hunting
Motor Boating, Canoeing, Swimming, Hiking

Store in connection, boats, motors, auto service
Guide furnished at request   Write for folder
Ice Fishing Open Feb. 1st

G. M. Whitten, Mgr.   ROCKWOOD, ME.

Maine Invites You ad, 1949. Maine Publicity Bureau.

McClure Store in 1930s, and Moose Head Inn (detail).
Collection of The Moosehead Historical Society #2018.10.0008.

The Moosehead Inn and Camps were managed by Randall Whitten beginning about 1953; he became the owner upon the passing of his mother, Zelda /Eldie in 1957.

Whitten's Store – Moosehead Inn and Cabins – Whitten's Cottages – Whitten's Lodge & Cabins

Rebuilt Moosehead Inn and Whitten's Store, ca. 1950. Collection of the author. *Maine Invites You* ad, 1951. Maine Publicity Bureau.

Whitten's Store – Moosehead Inn and Cabins – Whitten's Cottages – Whitten's Lodge & Cabins

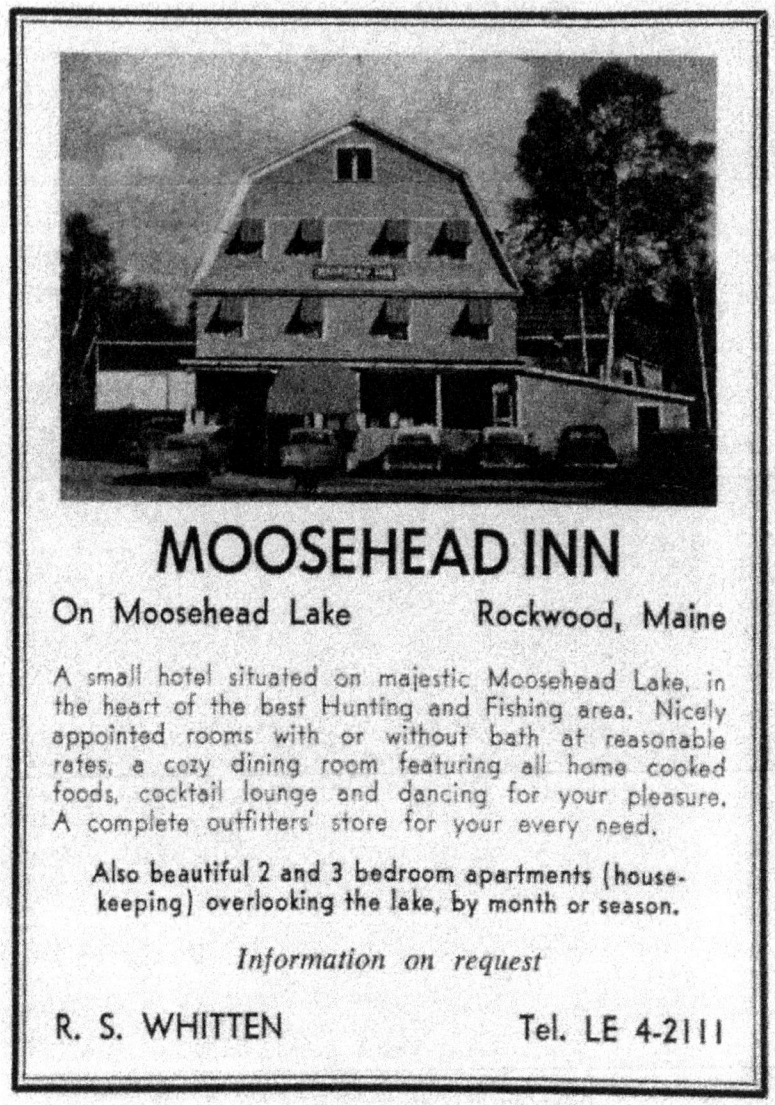

Motoring Thru Maine ad, 1953. Maine Publicity Bureau.
BangorDigitalCommons@Bangor Public Library.

Whitten's Cottages. Whitten's Cottages, on the north shore at the mouth of the Moose River, consisted of a main lodge and several cottages that operated from the 1940s through to the mid-1980s. Zelda/Eldie's three sons and their wives owned the property

Whitten's Store – Moosehead Inn and Cabins – Whitten's Cottages – Whitten's Lodge & Cabins

together. Guy Whitten Jr. died in 1983 and Mildred C. Whitten died in 2005 at age 92.

Maine Invites You ad, 1983. Maine Publicity Bureau.

In the ad above, the author presumes the Whitten's Cottage owners to be Mildred C. and Morton Guy Whitten. Deeds in the Somerset County Registry of Deeds show both Mildred R. and Mildred C. as being the wife of Guy Whitten, Jr. during the same timeframe, and the two must be the same individual.

Whitten's Store – Moosehead Inn and Cabins – Whitten's Cottages – Whitten's Lodge & Cabins

Lodge at Whitten's Cottages ca. 1980. Collection of the author.

One of Whitten's Cottages. Collection of the author.

These cottages were sold to Arthur and Reta Leonard in 1958.

Whitten's Store – Moosehead Inn and Cabins – Whitten's Cottages – Whitten's Lodge & Cabins

Whitten's Lodge and Cabins. In the 1940s and 1950s, members of the Whitten family also owned a lakeside lodge and cabins on the Lily Bay Road, about 6 miles north of Greenville.

Whitten's brochure (detail). Collection of The Moosehead Historical Society #81.1.3.

Whitten's Store – Moosehead Inn and Cabins – Whitten's Cottages – Whitten's Lodge & Cabins

Whitten's brochure (detail). Collection of The Moosehead Historical Society #81.1.

Wilson's East Outlet Camps

Henry I. Wilson, a Union Army Civil War veteran, decided in the late 1860s that an outdoor life in Maine provided a perfect opportunity for him. He moved to the Greenville Junction area and worked at the sawmill located on the lake's east outlet. (Moosehead's two outlets, the east outlet and the west outlet, are both the headwaters for the Kennebec River.) Wilson soon realized that the loggers needed lodging, and around 1880 his building at the east outlet location became known as Wilson's Tavern which he operated for loggers, fishermen, and those passing through.[50]

The family legend is that Wilson purchased a building located at "the head of the lake" and it was floated down the lake on a raft.[51]

The 1901 ad below described Wilson's building as an "... old and well-established home for hunting and fishing parties entirely renovated," which adds some credence to the idea that it was not built on-site.[52]

In the Maine Woods ad, 1901.

Around 1900, Henry built a log lodge with five cabin units that became Wilson's Camps.

Wilson was married to Maria (Dall), and their son Charles, one of their six children who was also a Maine game warden and a prospector, operated the camps for a time.[53]

Wilson's Moosehead House, shown above, had a parlor, dining room, kitchen, wait staff dining room, and guides room on the first floor, living quarters for the family on the second, guides quarters on the third, and quarters for the wait staff on the top floor.[54]

Harry's son Alfred J. "Fred" and his wife Vita Pearl (MacDonald) Wilson became the owners in the early 1930s. They had two sons, Alfred J. "Junior" or "AJ" and Donald H. "Don" Wilson. A.J., who married Ada Lawler, operated the camps with his father, and was also a guide and a trapper. A.J. tragically died in 1936, however by

In the Maine Woods ad, 1925. Maine Publicity Bureau.

drowning. At that point, his brother Don abandoned his engineering career and returned to operate Wilson's. In 1965, Donald H. "Don" Wilson became the owner.[55]

Wilson's East Outlet Camps

The east outlet dam (now made of concrete) was originally a wood structure built to control lake water levels and release water for the spring log drives which involved floating long logs down the Kennebec River to Winslow, Maine, and the Hollingsworth & Whitney Company sawmills. When wood was first cut for pulp, it was left as long logs and cut to 4' lengths at the mills. The year of general changeover to 4' on the Kennebec is unknown, but GNP Co. had transitioned to driving 4' wood about 1914. Pulpwood of 4' lengths was stockpiled along the shoreline, and during the winter it was pushed by bulldozers onto the lake ice where it would float once spring ice-out occurred. "Log booms" (rafts of pulpwood logs) were then pulled together by small logging "boom jumpers" and larger towboats, such as the *Katahdin*, would tow acres of the log rafts across the lake to the east outlet for sluicing down the Kennebec. In fact, for decades the *Katahdin* was kept at Wilson's dock. The last log drive on the lake took place in 1976, after federal and state environmental regulations were enacted to prohibit them for environmental reasons.

Katahdin at Wilson's docks.Facebook.com/MooseheadMemories/photos

Before automobiles were owned individually by families, guests traveled to sporting camps such as Wilson's by Maine Central Railroad trains to Kineo Station, or they arrived via steamers departing from the Bangor and Aroostook Railroad terminus in

Greenville. Summertime clientele frequently stayed a month or more. State Route 15 roadway along the western shore of the lake was completed in 1927, and travelers soon shifted away from railroads and steamers to the more flexible and personal automobile which enabled families to travel further in less time.

At its height, Wilson's had 40 buildings, including a 4-story hotel, 17 cottages, two homes, two sets of garages, an icehouse, a chicken coop, a stable, a powerhouse, two workshops, a large woodshed, a pump house for filling water tanks that distributed the water to cabins by gravity, and a motor house which serviced the boats. Depending on the season, up to five Wilson family members worked there, with the camp staff of about 13, and as many as 12 guides living and eating with them.[56]

Wilson's always maintained a fleet of boats with low horsepower in its early years. Similar to the other larger camps, it also provided one larger boat that could accommodate 12 or more passengers to transport guests to and from Greenville and Rockwood, and for fishing with their guides. An early morning task was to pull a string of canoes from which individual sports would fish when they arrived at their fishing destinations, and the guides paddled them back to the West Outlet camps while they trolled for salmon, trout, and togue. A noontime cookout was part of such trips. By the 1950s, however, guests began bringing their own trailerable boats rather than hiring a guide for a day or longer.[57]

In the 1960s, with the newly built Squaw (now Moose) Mountain Ski Area nearby, several cottages were insulated to accommodate skiers. Ice fishing and snowmobiling also grew in popularity. Meals were served until 1965, when a decision was made to convert many of the cabins to housekeeping cottages.

Wilson's East Outlet Camps

Wilson's launch *East Outlet*.
Collection of Donald A. Wilson.

There are now 15 cottages, all having views of the lake and surrounding mountains to the northeast and east and constructed with traditional screened porches. Cottages range in size from one to five bedrooms, and each features a well-equipped kitchen, full bathroom, electricity, propane gas furnace, refrigerator, all kitchen items, and beddings for move-in readiness. A boat launching ramp is available, and boats, motors, canoes, and kayaks can be rented. Master Maine hunting and fishing guides can be hired for hunting and fishing trips. The camp is also easily accessible to the ITS snowmobile trails and ATV trails.

Don Wilson fishing the river

The History of East Outlet Moosehead Lake, Maine, and Wilson's on Moosehead Lake,
   by Donald A. Wilson, 2006, p 23.

Donald A. Wilson, son of Donald H. Wilson, was born in 1941 and helped his father operate the camps until 1974. He is a registered guide and forester, and has written extensively about the Moosehead area.

Wilson's East Outlet Camps

Ice fishing. wilsonsonmooseheadlake.com

In the spring, a number of flyfishing enthusiasts come to fish the Kennebec River below the east outlet dam, which is limited to flyfishing only. The East Outlet Guide & Fly Shop located at Wilsons offers a variety of guided trips with experiences for everyone. For whitewater fishing in the Kennebec, Wilson's has two "drift" boats, one of which has doors making it easy for elderly (or not-so-coordinated) folks to get in and out of the craft. When the water levels are low, two row-frame rafts are used to get sports to those fishing holes on the Kennebec.

In 1974, after 109 years of continuous operation by the Wilson family, the Wilsons decided to sell but insisted that the Wilson's name be retained. Members of the Wilson family believe that Wilson's is the oldest continuing sporting camp in Maine.

Camp hosts are now Alison and Scott Snell, with Scott being licensed as a Master Maine Guide.

Drift boat. wilsonsonmooseheadlake.com.

Wilson's East Outlet Camps. Internet photo.

Private Sporting Clubs

In the latter part of the nineteenth century, men who were wealthy urban leaders in business and industry in the eastern United States sought the outdoors for their sports activities, primarily in hunting and fishing, and enjoying the camaraderie that followed.

Anglers and hunting clubs sprang up across the U.S. as the sports of fishing and hunting grew in popularity, and on Moosehead Lake at least six such clubs existed beginning about 1885:

1) Camp Comfort Club in the Sandbar Tract near Rockwood

2) Nighthawk Club on Sugar Island

3) Porcupine Club on Sugar Island

4) Spencer Bay Club at the Spencer Bay Narrows

5) Mt. Kineo Breakwater Sporting Club at the Mt. Kineo Hotel & Resort

6) William Tell Club at the outlet of Spencer Pond

Camp Comfort Club. The Camp Comfort Club was incorporated in the Commonwealth of Massachusetts, and located in the Sandbar Township Tract on the western shore of the lake just south of the Kennebec River's west outlet. The tract surrounds Lamb's Cove. David Fales purchased Sandbar Tract site in 1893 from Rufus and Mary Lamb, and built a house there. Fales then sold the house and property to the Camp Comfort Club in 1894.

The Camp Comfort 60th Anniversary Report issued in 1963 lists 16 members and five associate members who were primarily from Massachusetts, Rhode Island, and Connecticut. Club members' excursions from their residences to Moosehead Lake were typically for early springtime fishing in May and early June.

Camp Comfort Club, Sandbar Tract (detail).
Collection of The Moosehead Historical Society #95.4.238.

Much of the club's 60th Anniversary Report's contents show the compilation of the annual results of fish caught for many of those 60 years and the following data explanation was included to frame aspects of those logs:

> "Following is a list of fish caught as recorded in the log. It is not a complete list as some years no records were kept.
>
> – 1903, fourteen men in camp (3rd week after ice out), record says they caught plenty [of] fish, but number not recorded
> – 1904, ten men in camp for nine days, record shows one day's catch only
> – 1905, fourteen men in camp no record kept for four days
> – 1907, seven days fishing (3rd week after ice-out) no record kept.
>
> Early days many canoe trips were made for several days, record of fish caught not kept, etc.

The lists show average number of fish caught, per man, per day *camp was open*. However, all men in camp did not fish every day and many days no one could fish because of stormy weather. Therefore, to estimate the number of fish caught per man per day of actual fishing days, figures should probaby be increased by at least 20%.

The limit of 7 lbs. per day has also cut into the number caught the last few years."

1926 photo of 11 Comfort Club members (detail). Collection of The Moosehead Historical Society #95.4.238.

(From 1894 to 1908 the legal weight limit was set at 50 lbs. of trout per person per day. Increasing fishing pressure caused this limit to be reduced several times during the coming years, and in 1908 fishing regulations were revised to set the limit at 15 lbs. It was further reduced to 7½ pounds in 1942.)

Private Sporting Clubs

"Interesting items" taken from the camp logbook (1893-1936), which show the humorous side of its members.

INTERESTING ITEMS
TAKEN FROM CAMP LOG

1893—Land purchased from Rufus & Mary Lamb by D. L. Fales—house built.

1894—Smoke house built.

1895—First salmon caught by Hazard—4½ lbs.

1896—Camp sold to Camp Comfort Club by D. L. Fales.

1900—Brass cannon presented to club by John Booth.

1903—Hiram Ricker presented a case Poland Water to club.

1912—Judge Bolster's boat launched but engine refused to budge, for sale cheap.

1913—Guides struck for increase in wages from $3.00 to $4.00 a day. 2 quit—2 fired. Rest agreed to work for $3.00—handled on legal advice of Lawyer Stanley Bolster.

1913—May 13—Steamer Katahdin burned to water's edge.

1914—Judge Bolster sold his boat to Wm. McKinney for $25.00 and McKinney sold it to Guide Nesbit for $40.00.

1915—May 1st—5" snow in camp.

1919—Judge Bolster arrived ex-baggage. He exchanged his grip at Portland with one Mary Carden (whoever she may be).

1921—Last summer the camp was rented to Prof. J. R. Elliot of Bowdoin for $75.00. Before he arrived a thief broke in and stole all the best blankets.

1925—Henry Street took his 3rd dip in the lake—complained water too warm—temperature of water 40 deg.

1926—Camp rented to Prof. A. Waterman of Yale for summer months.

Camp Comfort report (detail on this and the following page). Collection of The Moosehead Historical Society #95.4.238.

Private Sporting Clubs

1929—At an alleged and probably illegal meeting somewhere in R. I. at some uncertain time during the past winter it was voted, we are informed, that the camp should be opened on May 11, 1929. In consequence thereof, the camp was duly and officially opened by the two Bolsters on May 8. S. M. B. Bob Stein towed a new float to camp.

1929—Commodore Ed. Harris was presented with an elegant watch chain (Came from one of the log booms) which he accepted with a few choice remarks.

1930—May 11—Governor's order bars fishing from midnight till it rains.

May 13—Went home—HELL! S. M. B.

1931—At noon Fred Kimball became slightly confused as to starboard and port and got out of the canoe on wrong side. He hung himself in front of the fire and at last reports was none the worse for the bath—probably better. The Polar Bear Club gets another member. H. A. S.

1932—May 20—Due to forest fires the state has banned all lunch parties ashore and all fishing from the shore.

1933—S. M. Bolster is reported to have taken 17 pennies from the commodore (H. A. S.). The rumor is that when there is a choice of fishing or taking money from innocent Elis, Stanley forgets he ever knew how to cast a fly.

1934—At the poker game, Fred Kimball asked the prize question of the week "When do the guests who are visiting camp for the first time clean out the privy?"

1934—Up until the arrival of the Bolster boys the Polar Bear Club had been meeting under the shower system. This proved to be too soft for them so the meeting was a regular one with a real dive and swim this morning. (Note: Temperature of water 43 deg.).

1935—May 20. Gardner Bolster left camp for Boston because some lady did not know glass was not usually served in pickle jars and was trying to collect damages from one of his clients.

1936—May 16. Temperature 24 deg.—very windy—trees and bushes along edge of lake covered with ice from spray—no fishing.

On May 15, 1960, the Camp Comfort Club members voted to sell their real estate to George Lamb and authorized club president Gardner T. Bolster to execute the sale which took place in 1962. Lamb sold the property to Louis Hilton of Greenville in 1964, and ownership remains in private hands.

Nighthawk Club. The Nighthawk Club camps were established about 1891 and were located on Sugar Island nine miles north of Greenville, about a mile north of Sugar Island's Camp Greenleaf. The club occupied a one-acre site leased from Milton G. Shaw on the island's westerly "thorofare" shore opposite Deer Island.

The Nighthawk Club was comprised of men from Bath, Maine. Prominent members were A.H. Shaw, a son of Moosehead region lumber baron Milton G. Shaw, and Fred Kimball, a son-in-law of M.G. Shaw. The club was the scene of much good natured rivalry each spring to see who would bring in the largest fish and members competed in other sports where men from business were set free from political and social pressure. During its heyday, some prominent and efficient guides were employed there, among them were Dave and John Brown, Clad and Irving Hamilton, Walt Taylor, Jack Masterman, Frank and Pete Tomer, Jim Perry, Sandy Johnston, Pete Turcott, Billy Brit, Ed and Jim Mountain, Dunc Matheson, Frank Auchier, Al Cripps, Joe Bouchard, Sandy Mullen, John Mansell, and many others. The club dissolved in the early 1920s.

Theon Heald purchased the Nighthawk Club lot from William Shaw in 1910, and the camps lay neglected until 1922. Heald founded the Thorofare Camps on the property and operated them from 1922-26. Ann von Slingluff transferred her Moosehead Camp for girls from the Nelson Camp at Moosehead's nearby Sandy Bay and operated at the thorofare site for the years 1929-1931. The Moosehead Camps, however, closed after the 1931 summer season. Heald died in 1930, and his widow sold the parcel, buildings, and wharf to Fred Webster in 1932.

Donald and Sophie "Barbara" Broadhead acquired title from Webster in 1944. The Broadheads created and operated the Wilderness Lodge and later incorporated the business as The Wilderness Club, Inc. The Broadheads added four acres to their ownership when they bought the adjacent "Hazel Point" lot and combined it with the Nighthawk Club lot. They sold the Wilderness Club properties in 1953, and there have been a series of owners since then. The Wilderness Corporation name has been retained, and the site is currently listed for sale.

Porcupine Club Camps. The Porcupine Club camps were established on a 2-acre parcel in 1900 (Frank Hall survey) on the easterly side of Sugar Island, to which was added a second, adjacent 2-acre parcel in 1906 (Elmer Bowley survey). The club was incorporated under Maine law on August 15, 1905, and its seven founding members were Joseph P. Andrews, Bath; Charles A. Coombs, Bath; Myron D. Cressey, Boston; Fred A.E. Dean, Boston; John A. Morse, Bath; Samuel R. Percy, Bath, and D. Howard Spear, Bath.

The club 1905 bylaws, give its purposes as "social and literary" which was the common definition for a nonprofit entity in that era. Its bylaws, contained in the book (courtesy of Virginia McCabe-Crumb) for which the cover is shown here, contain mostly standard organizational language, but does have a requirement that should the owner of a camp withdraw from membership, that member would receive for his private camp such sum as the directors were able to sell it for to another member. Article X required that, upon leaving camp, it and its furnishings must be left in a clean, tidy, and secure condition. If that were not completed, the directors would charge the member for the cost of any cleanup left undone.

The club may not have been sustainable, however, because it was offered for sale after only 15 years of existence. A 1915 sales ad describes the 4-acre property with four log cabins as being a hunting and fishing camp.

FOR SALE

Hunting and Fishing camp of the Porcupine Club on Sugar Island, Moosehead Lake, Maine. 4 log buildings, with private dock, and about 4 acres of ground, all heavily wooded. 8 double beds, 3 cot beds, 6 guide bunks. All completely furnished with linen, blankets, crockery, glassware and kitchen ware. Also 1 canoe and 1 row boat. Price $5000.00 cash. Possession at once.
Apply to W. I. Babcock, 17 State St., N. Y.

Recreation magazine ad, June 1915.

The Porcupine Club Camps were purchased by its Board member Captain Samuel Percy of Bath in 1919, and from that point did not serve as a sporting camp for sports or other guests. Percy owned the property until 1940, when his daughter, Eleanor Irish, received ownership as a bequest from her late father's estate. She conveyed the camps to Chester and Anna McCabe, who worked for Captain Percy, in 1944.

> *In 1894, Samuel Percy and Frank Small began shipbuilding in Bath, Maine, under the business name of Percy & Small. They conducted the largest business of any ship-building firm in Bath, building 28 schooners -- 10 four-masters, 12 five-masters, and 6 six-masters. They built and owned the largest sailing vessel in the world, a six-master named the "Eleanor A. Percy," plus a fleet of 11 large vessels engaged in the coasting trade, and employed as many as 250 men in their yard. Percy was a Bath alderman for two years, mayor in 1901, and a representative in the Maine legislature in 1904-05.*

Porcupine Club camp boathouse. (Note the "Porcupine Camp" sign over the porch.) 2021 real estate photo.

The McCabe family members retained ownership of the lots through two generations, until 2020, when ½ interest in the property and buildings was sold to Daniel Ross and the other ½ interest was sold to Peter and Cynthia Arntson.

Spencer Bay Club. In 1927, at the invitation of Maine's Governor Ralph Owen Brewster, Connecticut Governor John H. Trumbull came to Moosehead Lake. Trumbull's enthusiasm for the outdoors, particularly fly fishing, had led him to be a member of the Camp Fire Club of America, a national organization organized in 1897 to bring together hunters, anglers, explorers, naturalists, and individuals who subscribed to the principles of adventure and fellowship in the great outdoors, and to further the interests of sports afield and wildlife conservation. Trumbull was also known as Connecticut's "flying" governor for earning his pilot's license and his passion for flying.

Trumbull was apparently impressed with the quality of fishing in and around Moosehead Lake; in 1928 he had a 30' x 40' log lodge built to serve as a clubhouse for the exclusive Spencer Bay Club. Constructed at Stevens Point on Spencer Bay where Ervin G. Stevens leased 15 acres of land from Hollingsworth and Whitney Co., Trumbull's Spencer Bay Club grew from just the lodge to include a 15' x 50' wood framed building, a generator, water tower, and wharf.

Spencer Bay Club Lodge. Penobscot Marine Museum #LB2020.9.120.372.

Trumbull owned a 38' Matthews Sport Cruiser (shown on the right in this Spencer Bay Club wharf photo) with a 150 hp Kermath marine engine for use on the lake.

Spencer Bay Club wharf with Gov. Trumbull's Matthews sport cruiser at the right. ca. 1931. Collection of the author.

The author has been unable to discover any records relating to the Spencer Bay Club, but Amory and Elizabeth Houghton purchased the Spencer Bay Camps from Ervin Stevens in 1935 and owned them through the 1950s.

The Spencer Bay Club was located on land leased by the Houghtons from H&W, but its buildings and equipment probably were leased by Amory and Elizabeth Houghton in the 1940s. In a 1948 ad, the Houghtons advertised the "Spencer Bay Club" as their "discriminating resort for discriminating people." The same buildings and equipment description followed in the deeds of owners that followed until 1992, when Verdell ("Casey") L. LaCasce purchased the entire 15.25-acre Stevens Point site from Skylark, Inc., Scott Paper Company's land sales and leasing entity.

Private Sporting Clubs

COME TO MOOSEHEAD LAKE, MAINE

ENJOY A REAL VACATION at HOUGHTON'S SPENCER BAY CLUB. REST—PEACE—QUIET—a delightful spot, seven miles from any highway, on the wooded shores of MOOSEHEAD LAKE. Log cabins with modern conveniences and hotel service. Famous for real Maine cooking. A small resort for discriminating people. Boat transportation by appointment. Fishing excellent.

Write for booklet and rates

or telephone Greenville six ring four for reservations

HOUGHTON'S SPENCER BAY CLUB

AMORY and ELIZABETH HOUGHTON

P. O. GREENVILLE, MAINE

Maine Invites You ad, 1948. Maine Publicity Bureau.

Spencer Bay Club cabins (detail). Collection of The Moosehead Historical Society #2009.76.0011.

In 1992, Verdell ("Casey") L. LaCasce purchased the 15.25-acre Stevens Point site from Skylark, Inc., and advertised it as Casey's Spencer Bay Campground. The campground closed in 2020 and was listed for sale.

William Tell Club. The William Tell Club identified itself as the "Oldest Incorporated Hunting Club in the U.S.A.," and was incorporated under Maine Statutes as a social club in 1903. Located at the outlet of Spencer Pond, it was on land leased first from H&W and later the Scott Paper Company. In the first volume of the club's records, the secretary described its purposes as follows: "This club was originally intended as a home for the over-worked toiler, but it has now come to be a retreat for good fellows ... it is the ideal spot to rest and is beautiful beyond compare. Business is forgotten in the contemplation of nature and the sportsman reigns supreme." When it was founded, the club purchased, as its lodge, the clubhouse, furniture, and furnishings of its first president David M. Parks of Pittsfield, Maine, for $1,173.

The original bylaws initially limited the club's membership to eleven but were later amended to include more. The membership fee was $100, and annual dues were $10. In addition to David Parks, other founding members were Thomas Linn and George Babbitt of Albany, New York; Henry Estes, Auburn, Maine; Edward Lowell, Ezra White, Melvin Googin, William Newell, and Robert Hodgson of Lewiston, Maine; and George Parks of Providence, Rhode Island. Later members included Arthur G. Staples, editor of the Lewiston Journal, and Hiram Ricker, Jr. who at one time was the owner of the Poland Spring Resort, the oceanfront Samoset Resort in Rockport, Maine, and the Mt. Kineo Resort. Club membership grew through the years, reaching a peak of 40 members in the 1930s.

Private Sporting Clubs

William Tell Club lodge. University of Maine Special Collections MS 629 Box 3.

William Tell Club Seal/Logo.
University of Maine Special Collections
MS 629 Box 3.

Members made "encampment" hunting trips to the club for two weeks every fall, and guides and cooks were engaged to provide meals to the members during their hunting stays at the lodge. Mose Duty, the Maine guide and boat builder who started the nearby Spencer Pond Camps in 1901, was an annual guide for Club members.

The members enjoyed strong bonds of camaraderie, proudly purchased matching uniforms, membership badges, and adopted a Club seal/logo.

Private Sporting Clubs

In 1950, George Dulac, then owner of the Spencer Pond Camps, heard that the William Tell Club was closing. Dulac asked if he could take down the buildings and bring the materials over to the northwest shore of Spencer Pond to build some small camps there, and landowner Oxford Paper gave its approval (see the Spencer Pond Camps chapter).

World War II made it difficult to maintain the property for its limited use each fall, and the last trip to the camp by members was made in 1941. After the war, the few remaining members were aging and unable to generate sufficient interest to revive the club. It was dissolved in 1950, the buildings were razed, and the materials used to build several cabins at the Spencer Pond camps.

Traditional first morning flag raising.
University of Maine Special Collections MS 629 Box 3.

Private Sporting Clubs

Annual gravel pit picnic. University of Maine Special Collections MS 629 Box 3.

Deer shot. University of Maine Special Collections MS 629 Box 3.

Private Sporting Clubs

The William Tell Club's records for 1903-1938 were placed in the University of Maine's Fogler Library Special Collections. Minutes of the Club's annual meetings are available to researchers, as well as albums which contain photos of members' deer hunting successes, views of Spencer Pond and Little Spencer Mountain, and aspects of their life at camp such as playing cards, telling stories, and generally enjoying this annual respite from the responsibilities of their employment.

The Breakwater Sporting Club. The Breakwater building at the Mt. Kineo Resort served both as a sporting club and as the home of the Moosehead Lake Yacht Club, starting in 1908. The Yacht Club held summertime weekly races in competition for cups and other trophies and was a social center for its members. Almost no historical information is available about the building, except for the details regarding its architectural style that is contained in the application for nomination to the National Register of Historic Places.

Breakwater Sporting Club/Moosehead Lake Yacht Club 1908. mlyc.com

Private Sporting Clubs

The Mt. Kineo Resort's Breakwater Sporting Club/Moosehead Lake Yacht Club, 1911 image. Special Collections, Raymond H. Fogler Library, DigitalCommons@UMaine, https://digitalcommons.library.umaine.edu/spec_photos/240

Although The Breakwater was vacant for many years, it underwent restoration in 1999 and was listed on the National Register of Historic Places in 2002.

From the nomination form to the National Register of Historic Places:

"The Breakwater is a historic sporting lodge on the grounds of the Mt. Kineo Hotel and Resort. Built in 1909, it is an architecturally sophisticated example of a sporting lodge, exhibiting Shingle style and Italianate features. It was designed by Howard G. Chamberlain, a New York City architect, with funding from the nearby Mount Kineo Resort and the Moosehead Yacht Club. It was one of the centerpieces of central Maine's most renowned summer resort.

The Breakwater is a two-story wood frame structure, set at the southern end of the narrow peninsula projecting south from Mount Kineo into the lake. The main block is set on stone piers and topped by a shingled hip roof, with a side ell of 1½ stories that is gambrel roofed.

The primary facade faces the lake to the south, with a two-story recessed porch at its center, and flanking multiwindow bays on either side. A belt course of trim separates the first and second floors, rising in gentle keystoned arches above the windows of the side bays. A hip-roof dormer pierces the roof above the porches. The western facade is somewhat similar in appearance; the first-floor porch has been glassed in, and there is an eyebrow dormer above the porches. Windows on the first floor are twelve-over-one on the first floor and six-over-one on the second. The porch balustrades are diamond-shaped woodwork.

After a period of dormancy, the Moosehead Lake Yacht Club was revived in 1962 and is now located in Greenville.

Lakeside Housekeeping Cabins & Campgrounds

Although housekeeping cabins and campgrounds were not the focus of this book, a partial list of those lakeside establishments is shown here to give a sense of the scope and scale of their presence on the lake. There were many changes in both ownership and the names of the businesses over the years, and some existed for only a short time and evolved to single family ownership.

1) BARTLETT'S CAMPS, Greenville Junction. Ralph and Dorothy Bartlett, ca 1949. BARTLETT'S HOUSEKEEPING CABINS in 1950s.

Facebook.com/MooseheadMemories/photos

2) BEAVER CREEK TENTING GROUNDS, Beaver Cove. Beaver Creek is a stream that runs between Prong Pond and the lake. During the 1920s, Gerald (Gerry) Gartley traveled to logging camps, by way of horse, sleigh, or motorcycle, to bring "movie-shows" to the lumbermen. In 1942, he married Minnie Lee (nee Ligon) of Mayfield, Kentucky, who was one of the first officers in the Women's Army Corps (WAC's) during WWII. In the late 1940s, they owned and operated Gartley's Beaver Creek Camps nine miles north of Greenville.

Lakeside Housekeeping Cabins & Campgrounds

The camps offered housekeeping cabins and tenting sites on land leased from the J.M. Huber Corp., and in 1959 the Gartley's purchased the 10.2-acre site of land fronting on the lake from Huber. With the passing of Gerald Gartley in 1995 and Minnie Lee Gartley in 2006, the property is now in the ownership of Markham Gartley.

Beaver Creek Tenting Grounds. Facebook.com/MooseheadMemories/photos

3) BIRCH POINT CABINS/ BIRCH POINT CAMPS (from 1922-1947 was owned and operated by Allen Worcester as WORCESTER's) on Kokadjo Road, one mile north of Greenville. Erwin and Anna Chandler, Greenville, were owners from 1947-1969, and then David Strater and Janet Richards. Five individual housekeeping cabins accommodate 2 to 8 persons. Complete modern facilities with electricity. Dishes and linens furnished. *Maine Invites You* ads, 1948 - 1985.

4) THE COTTAGES, Greenville. Sam and Harmony Cheyney, 1950s and 1960s. Mrs. Frances Watson, 1982. Ten secluded, well-equipped housekeeping cottages.

Lakeside Housekeeping Cabins & Campgrounds

Modern, completely furnished for comfort and convenience. Screened porches. Gas or electric heat, and some fireplaces. Boats and motors for rent. Docking space. Gas and oil available. Good swimming at a beach safe for children. Situated in quiet spot off Lily Bay Road. *Maine Guide to Camps and Cottages for Rent, 1982.*

5) THE CRAGS, western shore of North Bay. Al and Elmer Andrews, 1950s. Fishing and hunting, heated bedrooms with baths, electricity, large living room and dining room with double fireplaces, boats and motors, and home cooked food. *Maine Invites You* ad, 1955.

6) CYR'S CAMPS AND HOUSEKEEPING COTTAGES, Rockwood. 1949 -1965. *Maine Invites You* ads, 1949 and 1965.

7) ELLIS' CABINS AND CAMPGROUND, Greenville, Leroy Ellis, Sr., and Ruth Ellis. In the 1930s, the Ellises leased land for their cabins and campground from the J.M. Huber Corporation through their timberland managers the Prentice and Carlisle Co. The Ellis family cleared the land and moved boulders to create a 1½ mile access road and the campground area. The cabins and campgrounds operated from the 1940s to the early 1990s. Cabins had cold running water, gas refrigerators, gas hot plates for cooking, and wood stoves for heat. Tenting sites had picnic tables, fireplaces, and there were some platforms. A camp dock facility was available, with gas and oil for outboards. Outdoors toilets only. In 1962, the Ellis family bought two lots (about six acres) fronting on the lake from the J.M. Huber Corporation in its Beaver Cove subdivision.

Lakeside Housekeeping Cabins & Campgrounds

8) GAMMON CAMPS, Rockwood. Charles and Julia Gammon, at the mouth of the Moose River, 1960 -1985.

9) GAUDET'S LAKESHORE INN AND COTTAGES (ca 1920s-1930s) and LAKESHORE CAMPS, Rockwood. Larry Crooker 1930s -1980s. On the shore of Moosehead Lake. Extra-large modern camps for the fisherman or family. Equipped with full bathrooms, electric lights, refrigeration, and every convenience for a week, month, or season. Housekeeping camps, central dining room, and library. Also, boats, canoes, motors, bait, tackle, non-resident licenses, guides, etc. Rest, fish, explore, photo, swim, hunt, or hike. 368 acres of privately owned land and wharves. A 1,300' runway for small planes. *Maine Invites You*, ads.

10) HALL'S CAMPS, Greenville. Cottage accommodations both on the shore and islands, including some fine log cabins. All contained fireplaces, baths, hot and cold running water, etc. Equipped to take care of from two to eight persons. Owned by Lawrence Hall and located near the end of Highland Avenue where there was a wharf, swimming area, and small community house.

Highland area of Greenville. Facebook.com/MooseheadMemories/photos

Lakeside Housekeeping Cabins & Campgrounds

11) HARFORD POINT CAMPS, Greenville. H. L. Davis, Proprietor. Modern, completely equipped for housekeeping, best fishing, salmon, trout and togue (lake trout). *Maine Invites You* ad, 1945.

12) HOTEL ROCKWOOD, STORE, AND COTTAGES, at Kineo Station, Rockwood, ca. 1910. Hotel Rockwood is at center and the store at the right. The hotel was popular with those coming by train to Kineo on the Somerset line, and the store was managed by William McIver.

Postcard of Hotel Rockwood (center) and store (at right).
Facebook.com/MooseheadMemories/photos

13) HYSON'S CAMPS, Rockwood. John Hyson, (camps formerly owned by Al Grover), on the west shore of Moosehead Lake. Famous for excellent salmon, togue, and trout fishing. Fall hunting, and expert guides were available. Comfortably furnished camps for housekeeping with all modern conveniences. Rates: $ 1.25, $1.75, and $2.00 per day per person. Boats, bait, tackle, and non-resident fishing and hunting licenses. 1940s and 1950s. *Maine Invites You* ads, 1948 - 49.

Lakeside Housekeeping Cabins & Campgrounds

14) JELLISON'S CAMPS, Rockwood. Alma Jellison, 1940s. Became Juke's Camps in the 1950s.

15) LAWRENCE'S CAMPS, Rockwood. Master Guide Bob Lawrence. *Maine Invites You* ad, 1993.

16) LILY BAY STATE PARK.
The Scott Paper Company acquired the H&W Lumber Company in 1954, including its vast timberlands. In 1961, Scott Paper donated most of what would become the Lily Bay State Park property to the state of Maine for a tenting and recreation area. The 925-acre park offers year-round activities and camping, and amenities include a swim beach, playground, two ramps for trailerable boats, boat slips, and a two-mile shoreline walking trail.

Lily Bay State Park is located on the eastern side of the lake, opposite the southeasterly point of Sugar Island. The state park offers two campground areas: 1) Rowell Cove Campground is located on the eastern half of the park and features 45 campsites for tent, trailer, and RV camping. Sites are equipped with picnic tables and fire pits. Some tent sites require a short walk from the parking area. Dispersed water faucets and vault toilets are also located around the campground area. 2) Dunn Point has 45 campsites which are for tenting only. A holding tank dump station is provided. The park allows walk-in tent camping year-round, but many amenities, including water, are not available in the colder months.

17) LINCOLN'S CAMPS, Rockwood. Margaret and Vance Lincoln. Five housekeeping cabins overlooking Moose River and Moosehead Lake. Boats available. In 1980 proprietors were Tiny and Eleanor Thomas and in 1989 Sharron and Maynard Drew. *Maine Invites You* ads, 1965 - 1980.

Lakeside Housekeeping Cabins & Campgrounds

18) McIVER'S LAKESHORE COTTAGES, Rockwood. Both of their lake-front cabins have a front, screened-in, porch view of beautiful Moosehead Lake and Mount Kineo. They are fully equipped for housekeeping, accommodating from one to five people. Each immaculately clean cottage has a complete bath with shower and a fully equipped kitchen. All linens and cooking utensils are provided.

19) MOON'S OVERNIGHT LODGES, Rockwood.

20) MOOSEHEAD COFFEE HOUSE AND CAMPS, later known as QUARTUCCI'S NORTH WOODS INN. Lily Bay Road in "The Highlands." A popular roadside restaurant with 11 housekeeping cabins.

Moosehead Coffee House and Camps.
Facebook.com/MooseheadMemories/photos

Lakeside Housekeeping Cabins & Campgrounds

21) MOOSEHEAD LODGE, Greenville. Howard Corsa, 1933 - 1958.

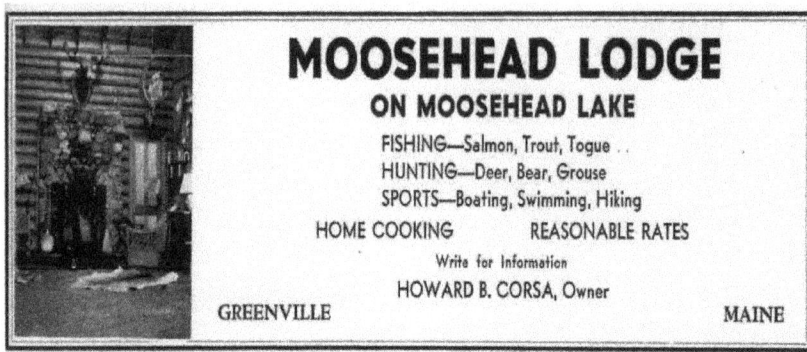

Maine Invites You ad, 1933. Maine Publicity Bureau.

22) MT. KINEO CABINS, Milton and Peggy Fuller, housekeeping cabins, 1980s.

23) ROCKWOOD COTTAGES, Denny and Patty Russo, and Ron and Bonnie Searles, 1980s. Open year-round. Fishing for landlocked salmon, brook trout, or togue, or flyfishing ponds, rivers, and streams. Hunting, ice fishing, snowmobiling, alpine or cross-country skiing. Whitewater raft trips, seaplane rides, tennis, hiking, or just relaxing. Shorefront housekeeping cottages offer clean, comfortable accommodations each having two bedrooms, fully equipped kitchen-living room, bath with shower, linens, automatic heat, and a screened porch overlooking Moosehead Lake and Mt. Kineo. Boats and motors, free docking, gasoline, licenses, tackle, guides, live bait, barbecue area and warm north woods hospitality. *Maine Guide to Camps and Cottages for Rent, 1982,* and *Maine Invites You* ad, 1989.

24) SALMON RUN HOUSEKEEPING CAMPS, Rockwood, *Maine Invites You* ad, 1993.

25) SANDBAR ISLAND CAMPS, Sandbar Island is 35-acres in size and located near the western shore of the lake just south

Lakeside Housekeeping Cabins & Campgrounds

of Mt. Kineo. One to four-bedroom housekeeping cabins with electricity hot and cold running water. Boats for rent, beaches, and water sports. *Maine Invites You* ad, 1955.

26) SANDY BAY CAMPS, 3½ miles north of Greenville. Howard and Myra Jackson, then Dave and Beverly Dupont, then Bearces 1958-1962. Four miles north of Greenville. Fifteen clean, comfortable lakeside housekeeping cabins, a campground, a restaurant serving home-cooked meals, a private dock, beaches, and boat rentals. Fishing, hunting, and family vacations. *Maine Invites You* ads, 1948 - 1985.

27) SUNDOWN CABINS, Rockwood. Patrick and Shirley Dubord. *Maine Invites You* ads, 1979-1996.

28) SUNSET HARBOR CAMPS, on Lily Bay Road, 2½ miles north of Greenville. Clarence Lang, owner, 1948. Eight secluded cabins on shore accommodating two to eight persons. Beautiful lake, mountain scenery, gorgeous sunsets. Cabins completely furnished. Automatic water heaters, flush, showers, electric refrigeration, gas ranges. Boats. Excellent fishing. Sheltered dock and bathing area. Four miles to village. Open at ice-out. Non-resident licenses. *Maine Invites You* ads, 1955, 1958, 1963 and 1965; *Maine Guide to Camps and Cottages for Rent, 1982.*

Reference Resources and Index

Research for this work would not have been possible without the resources available through:

- The Moosehead Historical Society, Greenville, Maine.
- https://digitalcommons.library.umaine.edu/
- Special Collections, Raymond H. Fogler Library, University of Maine
- The Hathi Trust Digital Library, a partnership of academic and research institutions, which offers a collection of millions of titles digitized from libraries around the world.
- MaineCat, the Maine Statewide Catalog that combines and links more than 100 public library collections contained in 10 large online library systems, all available through the interlibrary loan system.
- The Balsam Interlibrary Loan system for Maine Libraries.
- Registries of Deeds Offices at Piscataquis County and Somerset County, Maine.

---

[1] McCubrey, March O. *The Cultural Construction of Maine Sporting Camps*, UMaine Digital Commons, Maine History, Bowling Green University, 1994, p 116-133.

[2] Hunter, Julia A. and Shettleworth, Earle G, *Fly Rod Crosby, The Woman Who Marketed Maine*, Tilbury House Publishers, Gardiner, Maine, 2000.

[3] Ibid.

[4] Geller, William, "The Women Who Ran Sporting Camps, the Making of a Tradition in Maine," *Applachia*, Vol 72, Number 1 winter/spring 2021, Article 17, p 89.

[5] MacDougall, Walter, "Moosehead Steamboats," www.mainememorynetwork.net

Reference Resources and Index

[6] Ibid.
[7] Ibid.
[8] Ibid.
[9] Ibid.
[10] http://vfthomas.com, mainepostalhistory [based on Maine Philatelic Society records].
[11] htpps://enwikipedia.org/wiki/Somerset_Railroad_(Maine)
[12] Ibid.
[13] 1867 Report from the Commissioners of Inland Fisheries and Game, p. 28.
[14] Lowry, Nathan S., "A Historical Perspective on the Northern Maine Guide." Maine History 26 1(1986):2-21 https://digitalcommons.library.umaine.edu/mainehistoryjournal/vol26iss1/2ly.
[15] Doak, James M. and Doak, Tom. "Inheritance, Land Sales and the Future of Maine's Forests, *Journal of Ecological Anthropology* 13, no. 1 (2009).
[16] Arlen, Alice, *Maine Sporting Camps*, The Countryman Press, Woodstock, Vermont Third Edition, 2003, p 12.
[17] Weymouth, Dorothy Folsom, *The Crow's Nest, Camp Allagash, Moosehead Lake, Maine*, DWEL Publishing, Monson, Maine, 2007 p 5, 6, 7, 16, 24, 25, and 134.
[18] Osher Map Library, Smith Center for Cartographic Education, *Maine Wilderness Transformed, Timber, Sporting, and Exploration of the Moosehead Lake Region*, section II. Partitioning and Assessing the Land.
[19] Capen, Aaron III, and Worster, Louisa, *History of Deer Island*, ca. 1975.
[20] Weymouth, Dorothy Folsom, *The Folsom Farm*, 1999, p 16.
[21] Ibid p 17-18.
[22] Ibid p 11.
[23] *Bangor Daily News,* Obituary for Phyllis Kirkland Folsom, September 9, 2008.
[24] Wilson, Donald A., *The History of East Outlet, Moosehead Lake, Maine and Wilson's on Moosehead Lake*, published by Donald A. Wilson, 2006.

Reference Resources and Index

[25] Registry of Deeds, Piscataquis County, Dover-Foxcroft, Maine, compiled by researcher and writer William (Bill) Geller.
[26] Ibid.
[27] Ibid.
[27] Ibid.
[27] Ibid.
[28] Ibid.
[29] Ibid.
[30] Ibid.
[31] Duplissea, Shirley, *Hidden in the Woods, The Story of Kokadjo*, Moosehead Communications, Inc., 1997.
[32] Ibid.
[33] Registry of Deeds, Piscataquis County, Dover Foxcroft, Maine, compiled by researcher and writer William (Bill) Geller.
[34] Parker, Dr. Everett, *Beyond Moosehead II, The story of the Great North Woods of Maine from pre-history through the lumbering era*, p 21- 23.
[35] Ferland, Durwood J. Jr., *Kineo, Splendor and Silence*, Moosehead Communications, Inc., Greenville, Maine, 1996, p 1-22.
[36] Warner, Pete, "Married for 36 Years, Hunting Lodge Co-owners Are a Maine Outdoors Love Story," *Bangor Daily News*, September 4, 2021.
[37] Northern Pride Lodge website.
[38] Geller, William (Bill), *West of Chesuncook & North of Moosehead: Log Drives & Sporting Camps, 1830-1971*, 2021. p 11-13, digitalcommons.library.umaine-edu.maine history.
[39] Geller, William (Bill), *West of Chesuncook & North of Moosehead: Log Drives & Sporting Camps, 1830-1971*, 2021. p 14-20.
[40] Ibid. p 52, 53, 58, and 59.
[41] Parker, Dr. Everett, *Seboomook, from Native Americans to POWs*, Moosehead Communications, 2003. p 7-8.
[42] Geller, William (Bill), *West of Chesuncook & North of Moosehead: Log Drives & Sporting Camps, 1830-1971*, 2021. p 99.
[43] Ibid. p 106.

[44] Ibid. p 110.
[45] Parker, Dr. Everett, *Seboomook, from Native Americans to POWs*, p 23-31 (Northwest Inn, Seboomook Farm, and Seboomook House).
[46] Stirling, Carol, *West Branch Pond Camps,* 1967 Greenville Bicentennial Book.
[47] Howe, Anne, *History of Spencer Pond Camps*, edited by Christine Howe Black (c) 2020.
[48] Arlen p 141.
[49] Arlen p 142-143.
[50] Wilson, Donald A. p 16.
[51] Ibid p 27.
[52] Ibid p 11.
[53] Ibid p 17.
[54] Ibid p 12.
[55] Ibid p 18.
[56] Ibid p 12.
[57] Ibid p 23.

Reference Resources and Index

Index

Adams, Garrett	68	Capen, Alice	67
Adams, Joseph	68	Capen, Caroline Foss	63
Aguiden Lodge	97	Capen, Charles	13,64
Allagash, Camp	50-53	Capen, Gen. Aaron	63
Allen, Tedford	60	Capen, Henry	66,68
Annunziato, Richard & Kath	105	Capen, Norman	67
Appalachian Mountain Club	199	Capens, The	63-68
Appleton, John	176	Caribou, Camp	69-78
Atherton, H.A.	164	Carrier, E.J. Logging	123,124
ATV trails	43	Carry Brook	187,191
Bangor & Aroostook RR	4,17,64, 214	Casey's Spencer Bay Camps	208
		Chadwick, Lewis	197,198
Bangor & Piscataquis RR	17	Chase, W.A.	201
Bangor Daily News	74,152	*Chicago Evening Post*	5
Barrows, H.G.O.	157	Civil War	1,83,235
Bartlett's Housekeeping	261	Coburn Steamship Co.	11,13,188
Battery Point	119	Cochrane, Herbert	116
Beaver Cove Camps	54-57	Colarusso, Robert	130
Beaver Cove, Town of	55	Colbath, Martin	188,189
Beaver Creek Camps	261,262	Cole, William	128
Berzinis, Robert	130	Comfort Club, Camp	242-247
Bigney, Capt. Fred	50,51	Conservation easements	39-41
Bigney, Major Benjamin	11	Cooke, Jay Jr.	83,88,89
Bigney, Sam	137	Cooke, Jay Sr.	83,87,89
Birch Point Camps	110,262	Cottages, The	262,263
Birches, The	58-62	Coyote Ridge Guide & Outfiltting	212
Black, Dana	211		
Boom Jumpers	237	Crafts, Arthur	182,217
Boutin, Dale & Margaret	67,68	Crags, The	263
Bradbury, John	157	Crehore, E.	63
Bradstreet Project	191-193	Croce, Bob	210
Brattan, R. Frank	51,52	Crocker, John	157
Breakwater Sporting Club	167,258, 259	Cronin, Gail Johnson	94
		Crosby, Cordelia "Fly Rod"	5,6
Brewster, Gov. Ralph Owen	251	Crow's Nest Camp	50, 51
Bridges, Rick & Stacey	223	Curran, Nicholas	176
Broadhead, Donald & Sophie	117,118, 248	Curtis, Don	130
		Cyr's Camps & Cottages	263
Broadhead's Wilderness Lodge	117,118, 248	Davis, Vernon & Barbara	54
		Dawley, Florence	79
Brown, John	50	Day, Mary Starr Kessler	97
Canadian Pacific Railroad	4,17	Day, Richard	97
Candeloro, Fred	131	Day, Robert & Mary Kessler	97
Candeloro, Nick & Marie	133	Days Academy Grant	98,209
Capen, Aaron Jr.	63,68	Deer Island House	63,66

Reference Resources and Index

Deerhead Farm	161	Greenleaf, Harry	114
Dennen, Orrin	157	Guides	29-37
DePaul, Joscelyn	97	Gurney, F.E.	128
Destraz, Alice	145	Hadley, Craig & Kerry	68
Drift fishing	171,240	Hale, William Gsrdner	97
Dulac, George and Louise	209,210, 256	& Harriet Swinburne	
		Halls Camps	264
Duty, Mose	209,210, 255	Hamilton, Irving & Laura	128,190, 191
East Outlet Guide & Fly Shop	240	Hamilton, Vivian Harford	145
East Outlet/Wilsons Camps	239-245	Point Camps Haverford	265
Eastman, Thornton &. Marjorie	208	School	50
Eastman's Spencer Bay Camps	208	Hazel Point	119,248
Eckstorm, Fannie Hardy	7	Heald, Theon	116,117, 247
Ellis Camps	263		
Eveleth, John	13,14,134	Hilton, C. Max & Edith	164
Eveleth, Oliver	134	Hilton Timber Trust	68
Fahey, Oswald "Oz"	58	Holland, Bill & Nancy	201
Farm Island	41,217	Hollingsworth & Whitney	Many references
Father LaRoche	125		
Ferguson Point	220	Hopkins, Mary Alden	7
Finch, Annie	75,76	Horne, Glen & Sarah	212
Finch, Henry, Jr. & Margaret	75	Houghton, Amory & Anne	207
Finch, Henry III "Roy"	76-78	Houghton's Spencer Bay Club	252-254
Firs, The	145	Howe, Anne & Charles	210
Folsom Farm	98-101	Howe, Christine	211
Folsom, Mary	100	Huber, J.M. Corp.	38,54,55, 262,263
Ford, Enoch & Eliza Jane	126		
Forest Society of Maine	40	Hyson's Camps	265
Freyinghuysens, Adeline	52	Island #17	225
Freyinghuysens, Peter H.B.	52	Jellison's Camps	265
Gardner, Frank	65	Johnson, Edward Rice	90, 91,94
Gammon Camps	264	Johnson, Harriet	82
Gartley, Gerald	261,262	Johnson, Harry	145
Gartley, Markham	262	Johnson, Melvin Maynard, Jr.	94,95
		Johnson, Melvin Maynard, Sr.	76,83,89,90, 92
Geagan, Bill	152		
German POW Camp	194		
Gilbert & Coombs Camps	102-105	Johnson, Virginia Rice	94
Gin Point	68	Judkins, Charles	162
Gipson, Frank	135	Kealiher, Constance & Clift.	197,198
Godfrey, Bradford & Isabel	75	Keating, Ralph	189,190
Goodwin, Dan & Marylin	56,57	Keene, Ruel & Ann	126
Gray Ghost Camps	106,109	Kessler, Mary Starr Day	97
Great Northern Paper Co.	Many references	Kessler, Richard	75,77,83
		Kessler, Robert & Mary Starr	97
Greenleaf, Elgin	110,114	Kirkwood, Phyllis Folsom	101

Reference Resources and Index

Kokadjo	125-133	Medawisla, Camp	202-204
Kozlosky, Charles & Marta	88,94	Melton, John & Nadine	169
Kulp, Raymond and Eliz.	201	Meservey, William	113
LaCasse, Verdell "Casey"	208	Methena, Mark & Sandra	52,53
LaCrosse, W.T.	184	Midla, George & Linda	131
Lakeshore Camps (Gaudet's)	263,264	Miller's Training Camps	150-156
Lamarr, Lillian	209	Milliken, Elias	83,97,140
Lane, Ferdinand	187	Moon's Overnight Lodges	267
Lane, Marshall	187	Moose (Squaw) Mountain Inn	214-217
Larrabee, Asa & Caroline	70,71	Moose River	58,106,144
Lawler, Ada	236	Moosehead Camp	117
Lawrence's Camps	265	Moosehead Coffee House	267
Leased land	38	Moosehead Inn and Cabins	227
LeRoy, Shannon and Larry	202	Moosehead Lake Sanatorium	215,217
Lessard, Alec	187	Moosehead Lake Yacht Club	88,165,258
Lewis, Donald	215,217	Moosehead Lodge	268
Lewis, Donald, Jr.	217	Moosehead Trading & Trans.	175,180
Lily Bay Camps	139	Morris, Joe	175,188
Lily Bay Cottages	139	Morrison, Abner	126,127
Lily Bay House	134-137	Morrison, John	126
Lily Bay State Park	41,266	Mt. Kineo Cabins	268
Lincoln's Camps	266	Mt. Kineo Hotel and Resort	157-168
Lucas, Jeff & Barbara	169	Murray, W.H.H.	1
Luce, George	174,175	Nat'l Register-Historic Places	166,167,
MacKenzie, Frank	104,105		258-260
MacKenzie's West Outlet	104	Nighthawk Club	110,116
Maheu, Malcolm & Delores	105,		247,248
Maine Central Railroad	5,11,17,	North Maine Woods, Inc.	40,41
	18,65	Northeast Carry	11,12,16,
Maine Dept of IF&W Maine,	23,27		99,173-186
State of	7,11,29,	Northeast Carry Inn	182,184
	41,63,75,	Northern Pride Lodge	169-172
	122	Northwest Carry	187-195
Map, Sporting Camps Marr's	49	Northwest Inn	189,190
Indian Pond Camps Mansell,	140-143	Oakes Cottage	169
Charles	134	Oakes, Louis	79,163,164,
Mansell, Horace	134		169
Mansell, Osgood	134	O'Donnell, Roy & Louise	201
Maynard, Roger	147	Ogontz, Camp	83-95
Maynard, Walter	144	Ogontz, Chief	88-89
Maynard, William & Gail	148,149	Ogontz Shoreline	69-97
		Old Mill Campground &	
Maynard's in Maine	144-149	Cabins	105
McBurnie, Keith	219	Ox Cart Railway	173,174
McClure Store	228	Oxford Paper Company	209,210
McIver's Lakeshore Camps	266	Packard, Burton & Vivian	75,105,
McWilliams, Herb. & Clare	74,75	Page, Hiram Rockwood	227

Reference Resources and Index

Page's Tavern	176	Saunders, Gordon & Edna	50
Palmer, Arthur	50,51	Savage, Dora & Simeon	175,176
Pattershall, Harold & Esther	208	Savage, Fred & Abbie	197
Penobscot Hotel	173-175, 182	Sawyer, Charles	127
		Scott Paper Co.	Many references
Penobscot Hotel & Trading.	179-216		
Penobscot House	175	Seaplane Fly-in	109
Percey, Samuel	248,249	Seboomook & St. John RR	193,194
Perley, Henry, Chief Red Eagle	35-37	Seboomook Dam Company	192
Perley, Wanna Red Eagle	121	Seboomook House	188,191
Perry, J.H.	110	Seboomook Wilderness Campground	194,195, 198-199
Phillips Phonograph	5		
Piscataquis Exchange Hotel	150	Second Roach Pond Camps	202-205
Plummer, Barbara & Wayne	170,172	Shaw, Charles D.	111,123
Porcupine Camp	119,120	Shaw, Milton G.	12,110,134, 188,205, 247
Porcupine Club	248-250		
Prentiss & Carlisle	38		
Private Sporting Clubs	242-260	Shaw, William M.	110,116, 247
Progressive Era	4		
Randall's Camps	196,197	Sheridan, Julia Crafts	41,215,217
Raymond, Ed & Shirley	184-186	Slingluff, Ann von	44-47,96, 117,247
Raymond, Ed. Sr.	184		
Raymond's Country Store	184-186	Smith Farm	99
Red Eagle, Chief Henry	35-37	Snell, Alison & Scott	241
Reimen-Schneider, Wendy	131	Snow, Herbert & Frances	129
Rich, Steve & Pam	221	Snow, T.B. & Edith	180,182
Richard, Randal & Colleen	169	Snyder, Alethea	54,56
Richards, Jess & Jack	129	Snyder, Frederic & Anne	69
Richards, John & Frances	169	Socatean	8,9
Ricker Hotel Company	161,165 227	Somerset Railroad	17,65,160, 227
Rines, R.H.	164	Spencer Bay Camps	205-208
Roach Pond, First	125-133	Spencer Bay Club	252-254
Roach Pond, Second	201-204	Spencer Pond Camps	209-213
Roach River House	126-128	Spinney, Lilla Blanche	218
Robbins, Chandler & Anne	115,116	Spinney, Marjorie	219-224
Rockwood Cottages	268	Spinney, Russell	218
Rockwood Hotel/Store	265	Sporting Camp Heritage Fdn.	45-47
Rockwood-Kineo Corp.	164	Stafford, H.W.	110
Rogers, Fred & Louise	201	Sterling, Carol & Andrew	198
Rollins, Gov. Douglas	218	SAPPI, Inc.	123
Ross, John	176	Stevens Point	205-208
Rowe, Henrietta	50	Stiles, Gary	131
Salmon Run Camps	268	Stuart & Stevens	205,206
Sandbar Island Camps	268	Sugar Island Trust	119
Sandy Bay Camps	269	Sugar Island Camps	115,116

Reference Resources and Index

Sundown Cabins	272	West Outlet Camps	102-109
Sunset Harbor Camps	269	West Outlet LLC	105
Swigert, Mary	110	West Outlet/MacKenzies	104
Tarratine Post Office	141	Wheat, Alfred & Martha	225,226
Teal, Carrie & Homer	67	Wheat's Island Camps	225,226
The Birches	58-62	Whileaway, Camp	79-81
The Capens	63-68	Whiting, Richard	130
The Cottages	262	Whitten, Ed & Mimi Pratt	201
The Crags	145	Whitten, Guy, Jr. & Mildred	227,231
The Firs	105	Whitten, Guy, Sr.& Zelda	227
Thompson, Ellsworth	105	Whitten, Randall & Helen	228
Thompson, Fred	1	Whitten's Cottages	230-232
Thoreau, Henry David	117-119	Whitten's Lodge & Cabins	233,234
Thorofare Camps	117-119	Whitten's Store	227-229
Tomhegan Camps	218-224	Wilderness Club	250
Tomhegan Camp Owners	222	Willard, John, Jr.	60
Towle, Harry & Edythe	58	Willard, John Sr.	60
Treadway Inn	164	William Tell Club	254-258
Trumbull, Gov. John H.	251-252	Wilson, Alfred & Vita Pearl	236
Turner, Ralph	128	Wilson, Alfred, Jr. & Ada	236
Two Mile Island in Lily Bay	225	Wilson, Charles	236
Umsted, Charles & Harriet	171-75	Wilson, Donald A.	239
Vallant, Michael	116	Wilson, Donald H.	236
Van Skoik, Bert	111-113	Wilson, Henry I. & Maria	239
von Slinghoff, Ann	44-47,96	Wilson's East Outlet Camps	235-241
	117,169	Wilson's Tavern	235
Wade, Paul & Georgette	169	Winnegarnock House	176-182
Wallace, Fred "Doc"	50	Worster, Louisa	68
West Branch Pond Camps	196-220	Young, Bill	188

www.ingramcontent.com/pod-product-compliance
Lightning Source LLC
Chambersburg PA
CBHW050928240426
43671CB00019B/2954